Columbia at 50:

A Memoir of a City

Len Lazarick

To Peter Fronchot —
Best Wishes Celebrating
Columbia's 58th
Birthday.
Len Lazarick

ISBN 978-1-63492-454-2

These chapters have already appeared as a series of 12 articles leading up to Columbia's 50th Birthday in The Business Monthly, MarylandReporter.com and BaltimorePostExaminer.com from July 2016 to June 2017. The chapters have been slightly revised and updated for this book. All are copyright © Len Lazarick 2017. Comments and corrections can be made to articles in the series at MarylandReporter.com or by messaging Len@MarylandReporter.com.

Published by BookLocker.com, Inc., St. Petersburg, Florida.

Printed on acid-free paper.

Booklocker.com, Inc.
2017

First Edition

Dedication

For all the people who helped me and Columbia grow over the past 50 years, especially my wife, Maureen Kelley, and for all the hundred thousand children born here, including our daughters, Sarai and Rachel, and our grandsons, Noah and Owen.

Table of Contents

Above: A drone aerial view of Columbia's downtown looking west taken May 2, 2017 (Photo: Brent Myers © Len Lazarick). Below, the model of downtown Columbia shown to Howard County residents in 1964. Photo Courtesy Columbia Archives.

Chapter 1:
How the 'garden for growing people' got planted and grew

When I tell people I've lived in Columbia for 44 years, some say, "Oh you must be a pioneer." But a pioneer, in old Columbia-speak, is technically someone who moved here in its first year, 1967–68. A few of those 2,200 souls are left, and all can tell you of the first store, the first school, the first this and the first that.

But this book, which first ran as a monthly series of essays leading to Columbia's 50th birthday in June 2017, is not meant as a piece of nostalgia. Many books and hundreds of articles have focused on the first decades of Columbia, the land acquisition, the planning. The essays in this book are about Columbia as a lived experience that brings us to the present, with a long view of how we got here and how it evolved from the plans and, in many cases, was not planned at all.

This is called a "memoir" because it is neither complete nor unbiased. It is Len Lazarick's interpretation of Columbia's 50 years, or at least some aspects of it, fact-based as much as possible.

For most of those years I was working as a journalist here, reporting and editing for the once-great Columbia Flier, and then The Business Monthly. I covered politics, state government, business and the school board.

I love Columbia, but of course, as a critical journalist, it is a love fully conscious of the town's flaws and quirks; I am more critical than its most ardent fans.

As its visionary developer Jim Rouse intended, Columbia has truly been for me and many others "a garden for growing people." I arrived at age 24 and essentially grew up here; I made my living here; my wife and I bought three houses, thrived here, experienced disappointments and unemployment here; we had our daughters at its new hospital and now our grandsons were born here; we worship here, shop here, play here; I made mistakes here, had successes here, made many friends and a few enemies.

Columbia is not a perfect place or even necessarily the only ideal place to grow up and raise a family. But it was for us.

The Next America

Jim Rouse and the company that bore his name nicknamed this new town "The Next America," a name that adorned the Exhibit Center in downtown before there really was a town.

In 1977, as Columbia celebrated its 10th birthday, I penned the lead essay in the Flier's glossy commemorative magazine, "The People of Columbia," full of pictures and profiles of the people who lived here.

My essay was titled, "No Promised Land, No Next America: In the failure of great expectations, great promise still." I thought, and still think, it was a balanced piece, an antidote to the hype and promotion that sometimes afflicted the early marketing. Jim Rouse didn't agree.

"We didn't know you felt that way," he said to me shortly after the magazine came out. And, I was told, Howard Research and Development Corp. (HRD), the arm of the Rouse Co. overseeing the new town, canceled an order of 5,000 copies because of that piece.

In a way, these articles are an updating of that original essay about Columbia—the good, the bad, the mediocre and the mundane, and sometimes even the very good. Because they appeared first in The Business Monthly—one of the few locally owned publications left in Howard County—and then at MarylandReporter.com, the news website about state government and politics that I founded and run, they will be heavy on those things I know best: business, politics, government, education, health care, religion. But I will deal in later chapters with other important topics, such as environment, arts and recreation, where I've been mostly a casual participant and observer.

First some history: The land

First, we need to talk about the history. Probably most of the people reading this have little or no inkling of how Columbia came to be. They just work in its many office parks, or bought a house here or rent an apartment because it was the right location and the right price. Given the vagaries of Postal Service ZIP codes, some people who actually live in Columbia "new town" have addresses that say Ellicott City and Clarksville. Others with a Columbia address are holes in the

Swiss cheese of Columbia's 10 villages—out-parcels, in Columbia-speak.

Columbia was first of all about the land and what to put on it—the same question faced by Howard County's first real developer, Charles Carroll of Carrollton, the only Catholic signer of the Declaration of Independence. His country estate is still owned by the family and sits in the middle of more than 1,000 acres of farmland just two miles north of Columbia. He, his ancestors and his heirs developed what was once 13,000 acres—almost the size of Columbia—by selling parcels to people like the Clarks to build a mill in 1790 and then, over the next two centuries, selling off other pieces as farmsteads and home sites.

In 1962, 130 years after Charles Carroll died and was buried in the chapel on his estate—the last of the 1776 "signers" to die—Howard County was still a mostly rural enclave between Baltimore and Washington. Lopped off of Anne Arundel County in 1851, the county had just 45,000 people, with a few pockets of large-lot developments along two-lane Route 29: Dunloggin, Allview Estates, Atholton.

With the suburbs of the two old cities growing, and Interstate 95 about to open on its east side (and I-70 on the north later on), Howard County was ripe for suburban sprawl.

Realizing this, a Baltimore mortgage banker named Jim Rouse decided he could build not just a better suburb, but a real city that combined both city features and suburban life.

He already was constructing a planned development on an old golf course in north Baltimore—the Village of Cross Keys—but that was a village in the midst of an old city. His company also was one of the first in the nation to develop enclosed shopping malls. Harundale on Richie Highway in Anne Arundel County was the first such mall in the East, opening in 1958.

A new look for the 'burbs

Columbia could be a fresh departure from the suburbs that Rouse's mortgage company had helped foster after World War II.

The machinations Rouse went through to set his plan on course make an exciting story even 50 years later: Second-hand agents, not knowing whom they were representing, bought farm after farm for a series of dummy corporations. Speculation was wild about who was assembling all this land—ultimately 14,000 acres—and why. The secretiveness was deemed necessary to keep down the price of the land. Rouse lined up the Connecticut General Life Insurance Co. to finance the project.

Almost a year after the first purchase, Rouse finally announced he was planning a new town, but that proved to be just the beginning. Then came one of the most intriguing parts of the process. Now that the land was owned, it had to be planned, with streets and homes and shopping and schools.

In addition to the physical plan, Rouse had a higher vision. He wanted a social plan to make the new city work for people. He gathered a group of 13 experts in nearly as many fields: government, recreation, sociology, economics, education, medicine, housing, transportation, communications and family life. All were white men except for a lone woman, an expert on women's issues.

Remember, this was 1963. The civil rights movement was coming to a head, and the feminist movement had barely started. In the Howard County of that time, the men worked, the women stayed at home (or worked on the farm), and the Negroes, some descended from Carroll slaves, went to segregated schools and restaurants. This conservative but Democratic county—Democrats were the more racist party in Maryland till the late 1960s—had elected a group of conservative Republican county commissioners championing an anti-growth platform.

Those were the folks Jim Rouse had to pitch to for his idea of a "new town," and the flexible zoning to make it feasible.

Four goals

As Jim Rouse often described it, Columbia had four key goals that grew out of the social planning work group, his own experience growing up in small-town Easton, and the spirit of the times. In some lists, the goals are in a different order, but this one makes the most sense.

Goal No. 1: To respect the land. Rouse believed strongly that "there should be a strong infusion of nature throughout a network of towns; that people should be able to ... feel the spaces of nature all as part of his everyday life." The "towns" came to be called "villages."

Goal No. 2: To provide for the growth of people. Rouse believed that "the ultimate test of civilization is whether or not it contributes to the growth of people—the improvement of mankind. Does it uplift, inspire, stimulate and develop the best in man?

... The most successful community would be that which contributed the most by its physical form, its institutions, and its operation to the growth of people."

This was embodied symbolically in the People Tree (above) in Columbia's town center, which was erected as the symbol for all of Columbia and still stands there today.

Goal No. 3: To build a complete city. Rouse explained it this way.

"There will be business and industry to establish a sound economic base, roughly 30,000 houses and apartments at rents and prices to match the income of all who work there. Provision has been made for schools and churches, for a library, college, hospital, concert halls, theaters, restaurants, hotels, offices and department stores. Like any real city of 100,000, Columbia will be economically diverse, polycultural, multi-faith and inter-racial."

Howard County at the time had only a smattering of those institutions and none of those qualities. The schools were not considered top-notch, and they had just been desegregated, though the housing wasn't; one of the newer developments even had covenants excluding Jews. While there was a long Catholic presence, with Jesuit and Redemptorist seminaries nearby, most of the churches were mainstream Protestant. (This was before the great ecumenical opening of the Catholic Church in the Second Vatican Council, going on about that same time.)

Goal No. 4: To make a profit. This final explicit goal is often glossed over as secondary, but as Rouse would say, making a profit "brings discipline to all the other goals." It was also important to him to demonstrate that good development that was focused on the other three goals could make money if other developers followed suit.

As lofty and attractive as these goals were, Rouse's pitch was practical as well. Columbia would be a boon, not a burden, to the small county, which would at least triple in size if the town were built. The inevitable growth in Howard County's future, he insisted, was better channeled into a concentrated area. The housing density in the new town and the business parks that would bloom there would gain revenue for the county, more than supporting the public services needed, and they would prevent sprawl.

Not a burden on the county

Columbia would have its own taxes—a lien established by covenants on every property in the new town. The lien would help pay for all the recreation and community facilities and the upkeep of the open space that would wind through all the stream valleys, with bike paths connecting every village. Even its health care would be self-contained, run by a unit of Johns Hopkins medicine.

A crucial decision that later would be much debated determined that Columbia was not to be a separate municipality with a mayor, police, fire and public works; it would rely on the county for those services. Like all of Maryland, under state law the schools would be part of a countywide system. The roads, water and sewer would be built by the developer and then turned over to Howard County to maintain.

The commissioners and their constituents were skeptical but realistic. Lawyer Jim Rouse may have been a visionary capitalist, a liberal internationalist and a social gospel Christian, but he was also an inspiring speaker and a superb salesman who believed totally in his product. To use a word he liked to use for other people, spread out in syllables, he was "extra-ordinary."

It did not come easy, but after months of meetings and presentations, county residents came around, and the county commissioners went along, eventually approving the plan and the new town zoning in 1965. There followed feverish activity to build the infrastructure: lay out the roads and pave them, bulldoze the bike paths, set aside the open space, put up the first buildings, construct the dams for two man-made lakes.

Then on June 21, 1967, the date now observed as Columbia's birthday, the dam was dedicated for Wilde Lake and Columbia's first village. It was named for the chairman of Connecticut General, Frazar Wilde, who enthusiastically agreed to finance Rouse's plans. The following day "The Next America" Exhibit Center opened, and on July 1 the first residents moved in.

True believers in the goals
These first residents and many of those arriving in the next decade would be enthusiastic believers in Rouse's goals—the first three, at least. It was the right time in the nation's history to act on interracial tolerance and interfaith cooperation; and three years later, in 1970, the establishment of Earth Day recognized the growing environmental movement.

Rouse's commitment to integrated housing may seem routine now, but in 1960s Maryland, it was revolutionary.

The social goals attracted people from all over the country, especially those of a liberal bent. The Johns Hopkins commitment to a new style of health care—a health maintenance organization—came as the Medicare and Medicaid programs had just passed Congress, and Medicare was being implemented just up the road at Social Security headquarters in Woodlawn, where many of the new residents worked, including me for a year.

Some others of the new, highly educated residents worked at a then-little-known or -understood federal agency just 10 miles away at Fort Meade—the National Security Agency (NSA). The super-clandestine communications intelligence agency at that time had no sign to announce its presence. No Such Agency, some would say.

Rouse basked in the media adulation, and the praise was almost universal. There was substantial criticism of the new town's architectural blandness, however. The homes were pretty much what you could find in any suburb, but architectural allure was not one of Rouse's goals. He wanted market housing that would appeal to the average consumer.

Frank Gehry, now a world-renowned architect who early in his career had slapped together the Exhibit Center and Merriweather Post Pavilion, decades later would comment about Rouse: "I don't think his taste was very good. It was penny-loafer and tweed-coat. He was a God-fearing man who didn't have much of an art education. His idea of architecture was little cabins and cottages, and it was down-home, home-spun and small scale."

The chapters that follow will flesh out how those four goals turned out and much else that couldn't be planned or foreseen.

To make a profit

Yes, the Rouse Co. and Columbia would eventually turn a profit, but 10 years later than originally expected. In the mid-1970s the whole project almost went bankrupt, hundreds of Rouse employees were laid off, and Columbia's continued development required a massive infusion of cash from Connecticut General, which dispatched three employees to watch over its investment.

I began covering the Rouse Co. as a business in 1975 for the Columbia Flier, along with the school board and politics. No doubt this period of pain and strain had influenced my 1977 essay that debunked the rosy-colored rhetoric of the early days. The Rouse Co.

malls, well-built and well-situated in mostly affluent communities, were ultimately generating more income than Columbia.

This profitability led in 2004 to the company's sale for $12.5 billion to General Growth Properties (GGP), the largest-ever real estate deal at the time. GGP swallowed up too much real estate too quickly, and burdened by debt it filed for Chapter 11 bankruptcy protection in 2008.

The name of the once mighty Rouse Co. disappeared from Columbia eight years after its founder died, and long after he had left its leadership. The admired white stucco headquarters Frank Gehry had designed temporarily bore the name of the Howard Hughes Corp. (HHC), the land development division that was once part of Rouse Co. but had been spun off from GGP.

Then, in a creative repurposing, the building was gutted to become a Whole Foods organic grocery store.

Sitting by a window in Whole Foods' open dining area—a great place for a quiet, mid-morning meeting—you can look out over Lake Kittamaqundi, the plaza, the fountain and the People Tree, the same view Jim Rouse had from his office that was once just one floor above.

The only remnant of Rouse himself is a pair of statues near the water of Jim Rouse and his brother Bill, who died at age 61. They were commissioned not by the company that bore his name, nor the Columbia Association nor Howard County, but by his nephew-in-law, Claiborn Carr III. Clai was once married to Bill Rouse's daughter Kathy and worked for Rouse in sales and marketing, sometimes driving "Uncle Jim" around as he gave personal tours. Clai later developed office buildings in Columbia with Kathy's brother Bill Rouse, at Rouse & Associates.

After one of the statues fell over at the Symphony Woods office building where they originally were located, the sculptures sat in a closet for years till they were finally resurrected to their current place of prominence. Most people must wonder who the men are and why they are there. A small plaque hardly does them justice.

To respect the land

Looking out his office window and from his modest modern home on the shore of Wilde Lake, Rouse could see a project that tried to protect the environment—as that goal was understood 50 years ago. There are many more trees now in Columbia than there were when the open farmland first was purchased. Perhaps 100,000 or more eventually were planted, initially from its own Clarksville nursery, since Rouse insisted on landscaping on the lots it sold, as well as the streetscapes and medians.

The Middle Patuxent Valley is now a permanent nature preserve through the persistence of a naturalist who lived there—in exchange for greater densities elsewhere in the new town.

If planned today with the environment in mind, the streets might be narrower to reduce impervious surfaces—but where would people park those unplanned-for extra cars? There would be tighter controls on stormwater runoff, as well.

The ideals that informed Columbia's design have now become standard in housing developments in Maryland and nationwide, with planned open space running through the stream valleys offering plenty of habitat for wildlife. You're likely to see more animals on a Columbia cul-de-sac that honors the contours of the land than you might in a national park. The white-tailed deer just love Columbia and its gardens, and so do the foxes, who eat the mice and bunnies, but perhaps not the skunks. A mother skunk and her babies once camped out under our front steps for several weeks before the critter catcher removed them.

To provide for the growth of people

The original planning for Columbia provided for those institutions that might naturally evolve in any new development, but only after the residents had moved in. In the traditional pattern still seen today in other housing developments, farms would be converted to housing, then over time would come the stores, the churches, the schools, the libraries, the community buildings, pools and tennis courts. Rouse thought this pattern backward. Why not provide for these institutions from the start?

So as Columbia residents moved in or shortly after, they found shopping centers, pools and community centers, an interfaith center for use by multiple congregations, and land set aside for schools, if not the schools themselves.

"The most remarkable thing about Columbia is that it is remarkable at all," Rouse told a congressional committee in 1972. "It can and should be replicated and vastly improved upon in smaller and larger communities over and over again throughout America."

That was not to be, and rarely on the scale of Columbia, with the exception of such places as Woodlands outside Houston, inspired by Rouse in 1974 and now managed by Howard Hughes Corp. In many developments nationwide, Columbia's influence can be seen in the proliferation of cul-de-sacs, rather than the old grid pattern of streets, and the group mailboxes that were an innovation the post office pushed in Columbia to reduce costs. Rouse spun their inconvenience as a way for neighbors to gather and chat, enhancing community life—certainly a stretch of the imagination.

Where's the city?

As we look out Rouse's window, we may call this downtown, but what Columbia still lacks after all these years is density and a feeling of urbanity. The goal was: "To build a complete city, not just a better suburb," according to Rouse. Yet, it is hard to call it a city with downtown half empty.

The 1970s oil crisis, caused by an Arab oil embargo after the 1973 war between Israel and its neighbors, and a recession with high inflation, devastated Columbia's economic model. Housing sales plummeted, as did the sale of land to build those houses, a key source of revenue.

Columbia had a bus system run by the Columbia Park and Recreation Association—the Columbia Association, or CA for short (not the abbreviation for California or the medical shorthand for cancer). But the town was and is designed around the car. The oil embargo that created rationing and gas lines restricted driving.

The plan from the start was that as the town grew with apartments, townhouses and single-family homes, the land at its core would become more valuable, and more expensive land prices drive buildings upward, creating urban density.

Prior to the economic troubles, the original economic model envisioned Columbia's full development by 1980.

Thirty-seven years later, that last phase of urban development is finally underway. High-rise and mid-rise office buildings are again sprouting up on Little Patuxent Parkway; new urban-style apartment blocks have sprouted near the mall. The arts area in Symphony Woods around Merriweather is being redeveloped and enhanced with a flashy new stage. The downtown of a new city envisioned 50 years ago is at last taking shape.

In a speech in 1979, in a rare admission of imperfections, Rouse said, "There are a hundred ways that Columbia is deficient, lots of things that are wrong, but there are a thousand ways in which Columbia is far beyond anything that could have happened unless we had worked toward an ideal."

The Rouse brothers, Willard and James, stand modestly on the lakefront near the fountain and People Tree. Jim Rouse's office was on the third floor of the white building that now houses Whole Foods. Photo by Len Lazarick

Chapter 2:
Business: Downtown and office parks went up and down with the economy

It was an odd celebration, even for the honorees. In hindsight, the way Ryland Homes commemorated its long, 35-year partnership with the Rouse Co. in 2001 was ironic for both companies.

In the Ten Oaks Ballroom in Clarksville—at the far western edge of the Rouse Co.'s "new town"—the homebuilder that got its start in Columbia and built thousands of its first homes was saluting its patron and the provider of its home sites. Rouse, the new town developer that the 1960s media idolized, had propelled the small, home construction startup to become one of the largest homebuilders in America.

The baseball caps handed out that day said "Ryland Celebrates Rouse," and on the back, there was the cryptic embroidery "5K/$125M." It meant 5,000 homes, a quarter of Columbia's single family and townhouses, and $125 million in land sales.

While the two companies were described as partners, the relationship was really that of buyer and seller. Using the raw land it purchased in the 1960s, the Rouse Co. sold developed lots to Ryland, and Ryland then built houses on the lots to sell to homebuyers—and did it quickly and cheaply.

"Not too many companies have these kinds of relationships," said Chad Dreier, Ryland chairman, president and CEO.

The cost of the land
The relationship illustrates a key financial aspect of the entire Columbia project: Buy undeveloped farmland at low prices, improve it

with streets, water, sewer, shops and amenities, and sell it for many times its original cost. Buy low; sell high.

At the celebration, there was some gentle ribbing on both sides about the most constant source of friction in the relationship: the price of land. "We don't charge as much for the lots as we should," joked a Rouse executive.

In 1967, the first nine lots Ryland bought from Rouse cost $45,900 or $5,100 apiece. Thirty-five years later, residential lots were going for 20 times that amount or more.

Yet among the ironies of the 2001 event was that Ryland, now a publicly traded company, had abandoned its attractive headquarters in downtown Columbia the year before and hustled off to California, Dreier's home state. The departure from the planned community where the homebuilding giant grew up had disappointed Rouse and Howard County officials, but no one brought it up at a celebration geared toward happy recollections.

By that time, the Rouse Co. was about done selling building lots to single-family homebuilders. Not far from the Clarksville ballroom was the last of a dozen model home parks, where Ryland and other builders, some of them home-grown but smaller, had displayed their wares.

Three-and-a-half years after the celebration, Rouse itself would disappear from downtown Columbia in a $12 billion sale to General Growth Properties.

The two companies that created Columbia were among the dozens of companies that have come and gone over the years. But unlike the tech companies that have merged or evaporated, Ryland and Rouse left behind permanent structures in which people live and work, like the 1973 Ryland Valencia model in which this book was written. Later contractors have told me lots of corners were cut in these Owen Brown homes to keep the price down.

During their time, the two publicly traded companies were a visible corporate presence in Columbia, with executives (and their spouses) serving on nonprofit and community boards. The companies were generous financial supporters of community causes.

Shelter and jobs

While Jim Rouse preached his grand social vision of a "garden for growing people," those people needed shelter and jobs, shops and services—and the businesses that provided them. Those homes and workplaces were essential to the economic model that would make Columbia a viable enterprise.

As Chapter One explained, before Columbia, Howard County was largely a farming community with minimal employment outside of agriculture and retail. The smattering of residents in suburban developments mostly commuted into Baltimore, still a city of 900,000 people, 50% larger than it is today.

There were only two major employment centers in the county—The Johns Hopkins University Applied Physics Lab (APL), a center for defense work where, much like today, few people knew what they did; and the Route 1 corridor.

Fifty years ago, and still today, APL was the largest private employer in Howard County, now with 5,000 employees, working mostly on federal research projects.

Until Interstate 95 between the Washington and Baltimore beltways was fully completed in 1971, Route 1 was the major north-south route on the East Coast, and already looking seedy. Warehouses, junkyards and industrial operations were concentrated there, and just east were the freight railroad tracks that serve as the border between Howard and the neighboring Anne Arundel County.

Aside from Columbia shopping centers—more on those in the next chapter—the principal employment centers were planned to be in downtown Columbia and east of Route 29, ringing the edges of the new town's residential growth.

With few people living there and the highways unfinished, the Rouse Co. itself built the first office buildings on the farmland that became downtown. It put up a hotel there as well, before there was a market to support one, the low-slung Cross Keys Inn. The hotel later added the current tower, becoming the Columbia Inn, and then in 1998, Rouse finally unloaded the property to become the Sheraton it still is today.

The company slowly added seven more office buildings over decades, but it saved the choicest spots until the population rose and increased the value of the land.

The east side

For the east side of Columbia, the company followed the pattern of developing business sites for others to build on. The first business to build there was Hittman Associates, which at the time did environmental studies, later branching into medical and nuclear equipment.

Fred Hittman chose Columbia because of its central location and because of a promised lifestyle that would make it easy to recruit highly educated workers.

"It was more of a dream place at that time," Hittman told the Baltimore Sun in a 1992 interview. "But the promise for me was that this was a place that would attract and hold scientists and engineers." Hittman would become the first chair of the new Howard County Chamber of Commerce.

It was a refrain that would echo through the decades from firms large and small about the decision to locate in Columbia.

For years, "Columbia had more cachet than Howard County" as a business address, said Dick Story, the county's economic development director from 1993 to 2006. He recounted the tale of a developer who wanted his new office buildings to have a Columbia address, despite their Ellicott City ZIP code. Go ahead and call it Columbia anyway, Story told him. A postal inspector told them to knock it off.

General Electric: In then out

Hittman's modest industrial building was small potatoes compared to the major sale for the biggest parcel on the east side of Columbia to one of the world's largest corporations, General Electric. Rouse sold 1,125 acres south of Route 175 between Snowden River Parkway and I-95 for what was to become the GE Appliance Park East. It was projected to employ more than 10,000 people, manufacturing and distributing appliances, similar to an existing appliance park in Louisville, Kentucky. Imagine how different the Columbia economy would be today if manufacturing had been its core industry.

The five General Electric buildings in Gateway are in the upper center of this 1970s aerial photo with other industrial parks below. Snowden River Parkway begins in the lower left corner and goes up to the water tower. I-95 is in the upper right corner. Photo: Courtesy Columbia Archives.

Ultimately, GE only built four mammoth buildings on a third of the site, and employment topped at 2,800 in 1974, when the company closed the air conditioner plant. Twelve years later, it shuttered the microwave oven plant as it began importing machines from Japan and Korea. It finally shut the range plant in 1990 as it acquired a more productive Georgia facility.

The saga illustrates the vagaries of the economy and the fluctuating dynamics of individual industries that were continually challenging the profitability of the Columbia project.

From the time Rouse started acquiring land in 1962, there have been seven national recessions. The most devastating for Rouse's Columbia project was the 1973–75 downturn that combined the Arab oil embargo, high inflation and high unemployment. Land sales plummeted and Howard Research and Development—the Rouse Co. division that was building Columbia—would have gone bankrupt except for an infusion of cash from Connecticut General, original financier of Rouse's entire Columbia project.

In this book, we use Rouse, the Rouse Co. and HRD interchangeably, but most of the business was actually conducted by HRD, along with various other corporate entities, reflecting different financing and ownership.

The Rouse Co. bought back the two-thirds of the land that GE never used, and later, as GE pulled out, some of those buildings, as well. In the long run, while the 10,000 well-paid GE manufacturing and office jobs never materialized, Rouse used the land to create Columbia Gateway, which eventually would include one of the largest concentrations of high-tech businesses in the Baltimore-Washington corridor.

By 1999, Gateway would become a hot location, but it was a long time coming, 30 years after GE's initial deal.

The hot location

As difficult as the 1970's recession had been for Rouse's project, the 1990s recession was more severe for the Maryland economy because of the cutbacks in defense spending from the collapse of the Soviet Union ending the Cold War.

As the commercial real estate market struggled to overcome this, as well as digest speculative overbuilding from the 1980s, HRD sold only one measly acre of land in Gateway—for a parking lot.

"I aggressively sat by the phone, waiting for it to ring," recalled Ed Ely, HRD vice president for business land sales.

The situation in Gateway was so dire that an empty glass-and-marble five-story office building was sold to the county government at a fire-sale price, becoming headquarters for several agencies, including the newly privatized Economic Development Corporation.

Then along came Micros. The fast-growing company, founded by a graduate of Howard High School, supplied hardware and software to restaurants and hotels worldwide. Its 700 employees were scattered among several buildings in Beltsville. A few top executives already lived in Howard County, and "we felt [relocating there] could help our technical recruiting efforts," its chief financial officer told me then.

In 1999, it put up the first Gateway office building visible from I-95.

For a brief time from 1999 to 2001, Gateway and other Columbia locations were the epicenter of an explosion of fiber optics research, with Corvis the biggest player, employing 1,500 people at one point and raising $1 billion in its initial stock offering. Companies large and small were trying to capture a share of the photonics revolution, boosting communications and Internet speeds through fiber optic cables.

The movement was so large that we at The Business Monthly produced a special section for a national engineering conference in Baltimore on fiber optics in 2001, featuring all two-dozen Maryland companies.

Those that survived the end of the boomlet transformed themselves by merger or acquisition. Some simply went out of business. The Micros sign that graced its building for 14 years has been replaced by its new owner, Oracle, repeating the continual pattern where large high-tech firms eat small tech firms.

There are few large headquarters of home-grown businesses anymore. MedStar, the hospital conglomerate that occupies the newest downtown Columbia structure going up at Little Patuxent and Broken Land, is an exception.

Not only is the Micros sign gone, so is Arbitron, the once-thousand-strong audience monitoring firm for radio stations that was located on Broken Land Parkway at Route 32. It was purchased by Nielsen, which now has a much smaller presence here. The Flier building on Little Patuxent Parkway across from the community college, once the headquarters for a 13-paper chain of community newspapers, has stood vacant for years and is slated for affordable housing.

Long-time community leaders note the loss in corporate presence.

"The business community used to be very much involved in social issues here ... as corporate citizens," observed Pat Kennedy, president of the Columbia Association for 26 years. Now, there are a lot of "corporate addresses" and "absentee ownership," noted Roger Caplan, head of the Caplan Group, an advertising and marketing firm.

Not like Columbia

What's even odder about this long run-down of the business underpinnings of Columbia and its role as a key employment center for the region is that Gateway may officially be part of Columbia, but by look and feel it and the other local business parks could be anywhere. Their landlords and tenants generate millions for the Columbia Association lien, but there's little sense that they are part of Columbia at all.

The majority of employees in Gateway, or any Columbia business park, do not live in Columbia, much as the majority of Columbia residents do not work in the new town, as was the case from its earliest days. Only a quarter of working Columbia residents have commuting times of 15 minutes or less. Close to half have commuting times of 30 minutes or more. Living and working here, as I have been able to do for half my career, might have been the ideal, but it has never been true for the vast majority of residents.

Nobody lives in Gateway, except for a long-term-stay hotel. There is no mixed use, and but a puny strip of retail. Larger office buildings have their own cafeterias, or at least delis. Even with 25,000 or more people working there, pedestrian traffic is nil.

Even Gateway's street names have none of the striking weirdness of Columbia residential cul-de-sacs, drawn from American literature. Instead, they are named for American inventors and scientists: Robert Fulton, Samuel Morse, Alexander Bell, Benjamin Franklin, Lee Deforest. On any weekend, the surface parking lots that encircle the buildings are empty.

There is still prime acreage for sale in Gateway, and while the focus of Columbia's development has shifted to downtown, former

County Executive Ken Ulman, who guided the renewed plan for the center of Columbia, said, "Columbia Gateway has got to adapt" as well. Laura Neuman, who succeeded Dick Story as Ulman's economic development director and later become Anne Arundel County executive, agreed that Gateway "needs a mixed-use development."

"People like to live where they work," Neuman said, recalling her experience as a top executive of Matrics Technology Systems on Stanford Boulevard in Columbia west of Gateway, where there was a bar in the building, a deli, a dry cleaner, and hotels and restaurants that the staff used nearby.

Howard County began taking baby steps in revamping Gateway in February 2017, with County Executive Allan Kittleman declaring it an innovation district, and later kicking off regular stops for food trucks to encourage socializing there. But much collaboration between county planners, developers, landlords and builders will have to occur before Gateway becomes a vibrant mixed-use district. That will probably take years, but could face less resistance from Columbia residents than the downtown plans did—because nobody actually lives in Gateway.

But tens of thousands of employees drive in and out of it, a daily struggle for many. Creating a new entry to Gateway at Routes 108 and 175 was one of the more intriguing ideas floated for rejuvenation, perhaps correcting one of the worst intersections in Columbia.

A familiar setting

The room at the top of the old Rouse Co. headquarters was as familiar to me as any in Columbia. The modern chandeliers with parallel panes of glass are gone, the air ducts exposed and the floor bare, but the balconies still overlook Lake Kittamaqundi.

I have this visual memory of a late 1970s annual meeting of the Rouse Co. there, with top executives sitting at an elevated table, getting ready to start the meeting. One called out to me, a lowly business reporter for a weekly community paper, about a news brief that had run with the headline: "Rouse has bad quarter." Heck, it was just a rewrite of a press release, and maybe the headline did overblow the financial results, but what was the big deal?

The big deal that I didn't realize till then was that in the days before the Internet put everything online, stock analysts would subscribe to dinky local publications where public companies operated, looking for clues and problems the companies would not freely disclose.

The space once called the Kittamaqundi Room, and later the Spear Center, was long the scene of the annual party of the Columbia Foundation, where you were likely to see all the movers and shakers in town. It was the site of memorial services as well.

This was also where General Growth Properties, the Rouse Co. successor, in 2005 had unveiled some of the first illustrations of how Columbia's downtown might look. Afterward, Pat Kennedy and I would briefly discuss my book idea, he suggesting I should write about Columbia as a "lived experience," as I've tried to do in this book.

In this room on July 8, 2016, I sat among mostly old friends and acquaintances to get an update on the downtown plans that may, at long last, 37 years after the original target date for completion, accomplish the goal of Columbia's downtown as "a complete city, not just a better suburb," as Jim Rouse had said.

Other people had their own memories of the room, in mid-2017 an unoccupied floor over the Whole Foods grocery.

"This is where I had my prom," said Howard County Executive Allan Kittleman, who graduated from nearby Atholton High School as Columbia was being built in the 1970s.

That day, Kittleman introduced legislation moving forward the final elements of the plan.

"Success is not inevitable," he told an audience of about 150 invited guests, all previously involved in the planning. "We need to jump start the plan. ... We need to make sure this happens before we're all 95 years old."

The key is to make the new Columbia core into a place to live, work and play, built around the town's first public structure, a revived Merriweather Post Pavilion, Kittleman said. Howard Hughes Corp., GGP's spin-off, is calling this area the Merriweather District.

It combines apartments, retail, offices and public institutions in a walkable mix with a decidedly urban feel. Plans call for 6,400 residential units—up 900 from the 2010 plan—4.3 million square feet of office space, 1.25 million square feet of retail and a 640-room hotel.

Building a 21st-century city "is one of the reasons I moved here from Baltimore County," said Howard County Council Chair Calvin Ball. "'Revitalization' is the right word for what we're doing here," and the enhanced center of culture and commerce already in the works is "exactly what we need."

His council colleague Mary Kay Sigaty, whose West Columbia district includes downtown, told the audience, "If Columbia is only a great place to raise a family, what are we missing? How are we bringing young people into the community?"

Having lived here 44 years, "I continue to wait for the promise to happen," Sigaty said.

The cocktail hour reception was really a pep rally for the final implementation of the downtown plan. A key element, long planned but not much publicized, was a proposed $90 million tax increment financing, dubbed a TIF. It authorizes the county to float bonds based on the tax proceeds from future development to pay for infrastructure, in this case a 2,500-space parking garage designed to service Merriweather in the evenings and weekends, and office buildings during the day.

When the county council began holding extended hearings on the proposals the following week, it became clear why supporters of the plan needed to be rallied.

Speaker after speaker in two four-hour sessions decried the plans. Key sticking points were the TIF—many called it "a handout" to the developer, "a free ride"—and Council Member Jen Terrasa's push to increase the amount of affordable housing from 10 percent to 15 percent. That increase was favored even by some of those backing other elements of the plan.

Too dense, too high, too many

Over and over, the council heard people say there were too many apartments, they would overload the schools, the hospital, the roads; traffic would be terrible, like the mall at Christmas but year-round. The proposed buildings were too high (most of the residences would be seven stories and the few tall office buildings would be 14 stories). There would be too many people and too much density—though the amount of greenery and trees shown on site maps and renderings is more than is seen in downtown Bethesda or Rockville.

LaTonya Peters had moved her family to Columbia for the schools and pathways. "I'm very concerned with the urbanization. ... The density of this plan seems to have no limit.

"We wanted the suburban lifestyle. If we wanted a city, we had plenty of other choices," Peters said.

That sort of thinking runs counter to most of those who developed the downtown plan, like Ken Ulman, who devoted immense time and energy as county executive to enacting it.

"People want to live in cities," urban centers that are walk-able and bike-able, said Ulman, now an economic development consultant.

"You want the right mix. What's the scale; what's the mix? How tall should a building be?"

Ulman faced opposition all along the way. "I don't begrudge people's anxieties about change," Ulman said. But "things change while you're fighting change."

"We've had a great 50 years" in Columbia, said Ulman, 43, born and raised in Columbia and now raising his own family here. "There are a lot of places that used to be a great place to live," he said. "Folks assumed we would be one of those places," but "we've got to stay ahead of trends."

Four months later, in November 2016, the county council passed the tax increment financing. In April 2017, four local developers filed a lawsuit claiming the $51 million in the TIF for the parking garage gave Howard Hughes Corp. an unfair advantage over them.

Two renderings of the proposed Merriweather District. Howard Hughes Corp.

Barber Tony Tringali was the last original merchant in the Wilde Lake Village Center where he cut the hair of tens of thousands of Columbians, including the hundreds of children whose photos decorate the walls of his shop. Photo Len Lazarick

Chapter 3:
Shopping and retailing at the core of the Columbia plan - Village centers and the mall

Tony Tringali was a living fossil, a historical remnant of ancient Columbia. His barbershop in the Wilde Lake Village Center is not just antique; it qualifies for a plaque as a historic landmark of the Founding Father's plans.

Until his death in March 2017, Tony was the last merchant standing from those that had opened their doors 50 years ago for the first Columbia residents. Before the mall, before Route 175, before the eight other village centers opened, there was Tony.

Through thick and thin, he'd been there. In recent years, it's been mighty thin as the Giant grocery that opened with him and later had been expanded, and then was torn down in a revitalization of the center. Regular customers like me would have to figure out how to get to the shop hemmed in by construction fencing, mud and broken sidewalks.

"We're still getting people back," said Tony one hot August afternoon in 2016. Some might never return.

"Basically, I've had a good following for many years," said Tony. The walls of his shop were covered with hundreds of photos of youngsters getting their locks shorn. As we talked, he pulled out a fresh photo of three generations, grandfather and son standing with a young grandson sitting in Tony's chair as his father had, memorialized in a decades-old snapshot that hangs on the wall.

"I've done these people for generations," he said. "I'll probably do them for as long as I'm around." He died at age 73. Long time partner Bill Grady took over at this writing.

Home-grown

As a teenager, Tony and his family moved from Baltimore to Beaverbrook, a development that preceded Columbia. He went to Howard High School. "I used to play in these fields" that became Columbia, he said.

Gone are those other first Wilde Lake shops: a butcher, a cheese shop, a Rouse-backed community bank, an independent drugstore, a dry cleaner. Other stores, like a Hallmark card shop and a sweater store, moved to the mall when it opened four years later. There have been too many restaurants to name, and, of course, the anchor, the Giant.

"It was the best Giant they had when it first opened," Tony said.

Tony represented the original village center ideal. Its merchants were the commercial center of community life, with other essentials clustered around it—a library, a community hall, a religious facility, a swim center, a high school and a middle school.

Tony was familiar with the village center concept from his early years in Baltimore's Edmondson Village. Already part-owner of a barbershop in his early twenties, he wrote a letter to the Rouse Co. It approved his plan, and with a long-gone partner named Richard, he opened Anthony Richard, a barbershop with a beauty salon next door.

"I would do it again," Tony said. "It worked for me."

Columbia's earliest village hubs ultimately didn't work out as planned. Lifestyles changed, markets shifted, and every sector of retailing changed drastically to adapt.

A hub of services and community life

Shopping and retailing are the heart of Columbia and its villages. Without a grocery store, bank, drugstore and other services, a collection of homes is just a suburb, like the smattering of developments that existed before Columbia. In Wilde Lake, the new residents were pre-serviced—facilities were opened before there was the population to support them, as were the original neighborhood centers and pools. It was one of the attractions of early Columbia.

Wilde Lake, the first village, was a living showcase of the Columbia plan trotted out for the national press.

The mall, too, was central to the plan. As envisioned by master developer Jim Rouse, the mall was to be Columbia's Main Street. According to Josh Olsen's biography, Rouse, whose company pioneered the indoor shopping mall nationwide, rejected the recommendation that the mall be located near the newly built Interstate 95. He wanted it at the center of town.

For Columbia's first decade or so, the mall served as the center of social and commercial life, as portrayed in the 2016 novel "Wilde Lake" by Laura Lippman, who attended the original Wilde Lake High in the 1970s when it was still round and experimental. Lippman captures the social dynamics of growing up in Columbia and the role the mall played as a hangout for teens and adults as well.

Shifting lifestyles

Changes in the way Columbians lived were summed up in 1997 by Wayne Christman, general manager of Columbia Management, the Rouse Co. subsidiary that oversaw all the company's commercial real estate in town.

"Thirty years ago, Rouse created a city founded on a village concept ... to give the people a central core location ... along with open space and athletic facilities to help them focus on their community," Christman told the Business Monthly. "Now, with two-income families the norm, few people have time to use the village center like they used to."

There also were problems with layout and design. The first four village centers—Wilde Lake, Harper's Choice, Oakland Mills and Long Reach—were all inner focused, with stores facing each other, and their anchor groceries were too small.

"What used to be a state-of-the-art village center grocery store consisted of 20,000–25,000 square feet," Christman said. "But grocery stores evolve, driven by market needs and desires. Now a store [has to be] 55,000 square feet and have a deli, a pharmacy, a florist, fish counter, salad bar and other things that our stores don't even have."

Later centers all had larger groceries. Dorsey's Search Village Center, opened in 1989, and River Hill Village Center, opened in 1997, are designed more as strip shopping centers with easy in and out. The last center, River Hill, is at the fringe of its village at a major intersection, far from similar competition.

Over the years, the first four centers have struggled. Harper's Choice was redeveloped with a new Safeway and a more open, strip-like configuration; the Giant in Wilde Lake was expanded, before it was torn down. But problems continue to plague Oakland Mills and Long Reach on Columbia's east side.

Residents of these older Columbia villages felt abandoned by the Rouse Co. as new competition opened with larger stores not far away. Rouse itself was undermining these smaller centers by its own developments, beginning with Dobbin Center in 1982. The strip center was anchored by a Hechinger home improvement store and a Bradlees.

For its first 15 years, any Columbia resident with a major home improvement project had to drive elsewhere to shop. The opening of Hechinger at Dobbin Center was a boon to the locals, even as it spelled the doom of the hardware store along Lynx Lane in Wilde Lake.

The same pattern would hold true for the next two decades. Large retailers with chains of stores established themselves on the land that rings Columbia's residential areas east of Route 29 and competed with the village centers for business. These new stores were also a response to a changing Howard County market, as development occurred to the north and south. Columbia was no longer the only center of residential growth in Howard County, though it continued to have the greatest concentration of land for stores and businesses.

Ten years after Dobbin Center opened, Rouse developed Snowden Square with land it had acquired from General Electric.

Big boxes arrive

A new trend in retailing, the big box store, was giving fits to all those regional shopping malls Rouse Co. had spearheaded across America. For developer Rouse, if you can't beat 'em, join 'em.

Hechinger fled Dobbin Center for a box at the end of Snowden Square, 40% bigger to offer a wider range of merchandise. Anchoring the other end of the square was BJ's Wholesale Club, the membership warehouse store competing with many smaller Columbia merchants including the chain grocers.

"There's an unfilled demand for this type of shopping in Columbia," said a Rouse Co. official. Columbia residents "have to leave the area" to shop at these types of stores, he said. And of course, the new big boxes were highly visible along a major highway, located just a couple of miles from I-95 where the Mall in Columbia wasn't built.

In 1997, Columbia Crossing got underway north of Route 175 across from Dobbin Center with more big boxes—Target, Dick's Sporting Goods, a massive Borders book store, and more chain restaurants on the outer rim.

In 2002, Rouse abandoned the village centers altogether, selling the eight it owned to Kimco Realty Corp., of Hyde Park, N.Y., along with the big-box centers. The community-centered retailing of the town's early years faded in the face of market pressures and changing lifestyles.

(A residual effect of Rouse's precarious finances in the 1970s was the development of the Owen Brown Village Center by Giant Food's realty division in 1978. Later, Giant found it needed to expand its own store and create something more like a strip center.)

The mall

But Rouse still had the mall, Columbia's Main Street. Unlike the village centers, the Mall in Columbia was never just for Columbians. It never could have survived; it was a regional shopping center, and when it opened in 1971, it was one of the best. Jim Rouse wrote to one of his executives that the new mall was "better than anything else the company has recently developed."

Even young architect Frank Gehry told Rouse he was "overwhelmed." "It is the most beautiful covered mall I have ever seen," he gushed.

Initially many of the merchants were local, like the Bun Penny deli, one of the last survivors that finally shuttered its windows in early 2008. In its first decades, the mall was also a central place for Columbia celebrations, like the Ball in the Mall.

Jim Rouse at the Mall in Columbia in the 1970s. Photo: Columbia Archives

But over the years, the Columbia mall came to look much like regional shopping centers across America, many developed and managed by the Rouse Co., located across the street.

Local merchants in the mall were replaced by chains, often with the same product lines. Locally owned eateries were replaced with a food court, chain-run.

The mall was evolving from its earliest days. The original Hochschild-Kohn anchor department store was acquired in 1975 by the Hecht Co., which years later became Macy's. Woodward & Lothrop, another regional department store, was replaced by the national J.C.Penney.

In 2004, the Rouse Co. was sold to General Growth Properties, an operator of regional shopping malls, which were the major part of Rouse's assets.

The company that had nurtured the village centers and controlled all of the land use was out of the picture forever. There was no longer a benign developer with its own headquarters in the middle of town guiding the process. For the first 40 years, Rouse had decided where the stores and offices would be built, where the neighborhood and community centers would go, where the schools and athletic facilities would be located, even where the worship spaces could be built.

Even when Columbians rose up in opposition to its development plans, the key decision makers were close at hand.

But, just four years into the new century, that benign developer was gone. Most of the residential land had been sold as lots, now owned by thousands of homeowners and hundreds of landlords. The business parks, once overseen by a developer with a stake in building community, were now in the hands of many. As the economy waxed and waned, the properties were bought and sold, some turning over multiple times.

Problems at the older centers

The problems that plagued the old centers did not go away when Rouse left the scene; they just came under new management.

While all five of the older village centers had their problems, few were in worse shape than Oakland Mills and Long Reach.

From the day it opened, Oakland Mills was doomed to be a hidden marketplace. The center was built in the wrong place.

Nearby residents want to believe otherwise, but the center is difficult to find, and sits on no major thoroughfare. It probably should have been built on Route 175. (The same could be said for Long Reach.)

Compounding a fundamental error in real estate development—a bad location—Rouse first built a mini-enclosed mall, with a grocery that was far too small. Pantry Pride gave way to a Giant that eventually closed. The old center was shut down and redeveloped into the strip center we know today, anchored by Metro Food Market. That eventually failed as well, leaving the space vacant for more than two years.

Finally, Food Lion agreed to take the space. Residents cheered.

Jeff Metzger, publisher of Food World, a supermarket trade journal based in Columbia, was dubious.

"I would say opening a grocery store [there] no matter who operates it is a risk," Metzger told the Baltimore Sun in 2003. "I just think that's a poor location. It has nothing to do with the quality of the retailer. ... The demographics [there] aren't particularly strong. [The area is] really land-locked, [and] there's no access to any major road."

The wonder is that any supermarket is still open in that location. A shopper with agoraphobia could find some peace there, with empty aisles all to himself and checkout with no lines to speak of. The Food Lion closed Sept. 16, 2016, to reopen as a Weis Markets store Sept. 23, the fifth food chain to try to make a go of Oakland Mills.

A large Exxon station next to the center closed in 1999. Its 1.7 acres covered in aging asphalt have sat vacant now for 18 years. Multiple proposals have fallen by the wayside, including County Executive Ken Ulman's promise for the county to purchase part of a planned condominium office building that never got off the ground.

Many chances to eat

The restaurant scene in Oakland Mills is almost an exaggerated parody of the vicious turnover typical in the trade. A frequently quoted statistic from the National Restaurant Association is that 60,000 restaurants open each year, while 50,000 close, for various reasons.

An early cover story I did for the Columbia Flier showed what a brutal and complicated business this can be seven days a week, from purchasing the ingredients, to preparing them and delivering them to table. Getting it right every day is hard to do, which is why chains and the formulas they maintain have come to dominate.

Because restaurant spots come with kitchens and bars, they tend to remain restaurants. So it is in Oakland Mills. Let us count the names: Long's Vineyard, The Crackpot, Phase Three, Barnums, Skipjack's, Channing's Crab House, Last Chance (which wasn't) and now the Second Chance Saloon. Other longtime survivors that have seen the anchors go and come are Vennari's Pizza and Lucky's China Inn.

While Oakland Mills may have persistent troubles, it at least has traffic and surviving merchants with food to sell. The poor Long Reach Village Center is effectively a zombie, walking dead to all appearances. Opened in 1974, the Safeway doubled in size in 1998 but shuttered in 2011; the Asian food market that replaced it stopped paying rent and was evicted. There has been no anchor for years. Half the storefronts are empty, the eateries are long gone, and its most active merchants appear to be a liquor store and a Subway.

Kimco had unloaded the center in 2004 to another out-of-state firm. After the anchor store went empty, the situation was so bad that the county purchased the center to revitalize. Consultants were hired, work groups were formed and several community meetings were held. Finally, on May 2, 2017, County Executive Allan Kittleman announced that Orchard Development would be taking the center off the county's hands and redeveloping it with apartments, a food court, senior living, medical offices and townhouses. And no supermarket.

Long Reach residents have long since found other places to shop. There is a Giant in what was once a movie complex across Rt. 108, the nearby Target or Wal-Mart along Dobbin Road, BJ's and now the massive Wegmans on the site of what was once a warehouse and offices (and the soundstage for "The Wire"). Wegmans, with its shops within a store for baked goods, meat, cheese, fish and prepared foods, is a megastore much larger than the other chain groceries it aggressively competes with. And for those willing to brave snarly traffic and long lines for cheap gas, a Costco warehouse store is only two miles away.

Remembering the restaurants

The various Facebook pages dedicated to remembering Columbia or discussing its future are evidence of how important an eatery or a watering hole can be. A community may chat in the grocery stores, but it builds relationships over food and drink.

Longtime Columbia residents have their favorites. There have been few neighborhood bars and eateries as beloved as JK's Pub on Lynx Lane in Wilde Lake, a knock-off of a British pub that opened in 1978 with a dark wood bar, antique mirrors and down-home cooking.

I would often walk across the fields of Wilde Lake Middle School from the Columbia Flier building on Little Patuxent Parkway for a lunch of specially bought liverwurst and onion on rye with a glass of rosé. It was the kind of place where you saw people you knew—lawyers, politicos, and for Friday happy hour, groups of teachers from nearby schools. Everybody didn't know your name, but many people did, all presided over by John and Claire Lea.

JK, a former university speech professor always ready to declaim, sold the operation in late 1994, complaining of 70–80-hour work weeks, the familiar lament of many restaurateurs.

"Sometimes it seemed like I was working around the clock," Lea told The Business Monthly. "This is a younger person's job—it's very demanding, There's always something you should be doing."

And then of course there's Clyde's, the grand old man of Columbia's eateries and a glaring exception to the turnover in the restaurant trade. I covered its crowded opening party in 1975, with its layout much as it is today. My story made note of the $2.50 hamburger and $1.40 glass of wine, which seemed a bit pricey to me then, but is pretty laughable today. My publisher reminded me that I was a business reporter, not a restaurant critic. For decades, it was the place for the power lunch and the let's-talk-shop-over-drinks happy hour.

The banks

Banking is one of those essential services that any thriving community should have, and was a key component of any village center.

It's been more than 40 years since I opened my wife's and my joint account with Columbia Bank & Trust, a company founded here with Rouse backing. I've never moved that account, but with mergers and acquisitions, we've had four banks since then. In succession, the bank was named Equitable, Maryland National Bank, NationsBank, and now for many years, Bank of America. We've gone from deposits in a small-town bank to one of the behemoths too big to fail.

This reflects the enormous consolidation the industry has gone through, said Mary Ann Scully, president of Howard Bank. It services my business account but is temporarily without a branch in a Columbia ZIP code.

Howard Bank is pretty much what's left of community banking here. Most other banks, including another home-grown, Columbia Bank, where my business has a credit card, is owned by out-of-state holding companies.

"Everybody wants to be a community bank," said Scully, but "it's probably not been executed very well. Poor execution hurts the not-for-profits and small businesses." The not-for-profits "get a bigger share of the dollars at community banks."

Howard Bank once had a branch in Hickory Ridge, where I opened my account, but "we're going to vote with our feet by having a branch in Little Patuxent Square," the shiny Costello Construction high-rise directly across from a mall parking garage.

"It is important that Columbia reach the Jim Rouse vision" of an urban environment to remain competitive for businesses and talent, Scully said. "If not, we lose our young people and lose our businesses.

"Having a more urban environment is very important," which is why Howard Bank has supported the downtown Columbia revitalization plans. "Some banks think it's political" to support the plans, Scully said, "but we believe that banks should be community leaders."

Of course, who actually goes into a bank these days, as people did in Columbia's early days, to deposit paychecks and get cash? Most transactions are now handled by ATMs and online, and even grocery stores dispense cash.

David's Natural Market

Revitalization has its costs. In Wilde Lake Village Center, barber Tony Tringali was not the only surviving victim of its struggles as Kimco demolished the old Giant and a third of the village green.

David London was 27 when he took over his parents' decade-old natural food store in 1986, turning Nature's Cupboard of Love into David's Natural Food Market. David, a graduate of Wilde Lake High, grew up working in the natural foods business.

His store at the end of Lynx Lane expanded six or seven times over the years, going from 1,000 square feet to 12,000 square feet, taking over space once occupied by Duron and JK's Pub. "We got to grow with the community."

The village center "was a great concept when they first developed it," David said, so that residents could "do their shopping in their own neighborhood."

But people changed, and they wanted to do their shopping "quickly," gravitating to "more strip-type centers."

When Kimco proposed redeveloping Wilde Lake with 250 new apartments, five stories high, and without a traditional grocery, local residents were up in arms. They wanted a grocery the way Rouse had planned, even though Kimco insisted no chain would locate there.

But David bought the concept, and planned a fine new market for his organic foods and herbal products that would anchor the center, along with a shiny bright CVS drugstore.

At first, he was told Lynx Lane would be closed for two weeks for the construction, but that dragged out into nine months. Customers had trouble figuring out how to find the old store. The new market was to have opened in March 2014, with brand new equipment, but it actually wouldn't greet customers till eight months later.

"It's just killing us," David said in a 2016 interview. "We lost 30% of our business, and we haven't gotten it back yet."

While the months dragged on, the new Whole Foods opened in the former Rouse Co. headquarters less than two miles away. But David said he doesn't see it as a competitor.

"We try to offer more personalized service," David said. "All my employees have been there for a long time," like Barbara Wright, the chef manager of the health foods cafe who had worked the kitchen at JK's Pub.

"We're local; we're part of the community," David said.

But in retrospect, "it was a lot more money than I thought," he said. "It would have been easier to open a new store than to move it."

He said it may take as long as 10 years to recoup the investment. "Thank goodness I had two other stores," one in Gambrills and a second in Forest Hill, Harford County.

"I think it will be OK," especially as renters occupy the apartments next door, David said.

A similar redevelopment process has been proposed for the Hickory Ridge Village Center that opened in 1992, with Kimco proposing the addition of an apartment block. The current Giant would stay, but the retail stores that face it on a courtyard would be relocated around the parking area, at least temporarily putting them out of business.

The changes contemplated led the owners of the gem of a small Italian neighborhood restaurant, Luna Bella Ristorante, to close late in 2016, with a long lament on its Facebook page by co-owner Celeste Gebler.

"If nothing else comes out of this, I hope this can help the lives of other small business owners. I hope that large corporations will start to look at us as though we matter more. Perhaps you can share with them that we change lives. We don't need to fill our pockets with stuff … we need to fill our hearts with the 'stuff' that makes us real. Tell them this in your community meetings."

It's a lament other merchants could share.

Barber Tony Tringali, on the other hand, who had his struggles with Kimco and Rouse's Columbia Management before that, had been hopeful about the future. "Every place you look out here you see a crane," said Tony. "I don't see why we can't get our fair share" of business from the new residents.

The rebuilt David's Natural Market with the new Alta Wilde Lake Apartments in the background at the renovated village center. Photo: Len Lazarick

Chapter 4:
Media: Communications part of building community

Tom Graham's decision to move from the Howard County Times to the Columbia Flier was a bit puzzling to me as I visited him and the new planned community for the first time in early 1973.

After 14 months, Tom was leaving the well-established Times that looked like a traditional newspaper for the magazine-sized Columbia startup that looked liked it came out of a typewriter—because it did.

It turned out to be a smart decision that gave Tom a quarter-century of employment, opportunity and influence. He was attracted by the enthusiasm of the new editor, Jean Moon. Jean said she recognized that Tom was better at reporting on zoning than she was, and she also offered a small raise.

"Despite that, I didn't say yes until I had a face-to-face with Zeke Orlinsky, the publisher," Tom said. Tom's future wife, Mary Kay Sigaty, "was working as a bank teller at the time, and she had warned me that the Flier's checks sometimes bounced. When I asked him about this, Zeke said that would never be a problem with my paycheck, and it wasn't."

Maureen Kelley and I moved to Columbia a few months later, in June 1973. Maureen, newly graduated from nursing school at Boston College, where all four of us had met, got a job as a visiting nurse on her first interview. I got a job with another newspaper in town, Columbia Life, which was supposedly "recapitalizing."

Columbia Life survived for another issue or two and then died without a trace. I sued the publisher for pay. All I got was an office desk and chair.

Other newspapers have come and gone—Columbia Villager, the News Columbian (an edition of the conservative Central Maryland News), the Columbia Times (an edition of the Howard County Times), and a bit later, the Columbia Forum. In the following decades, dailies would enter the local market with the Howard Sun and the Post's Howard Weekly. There were other publications along the way, The Business Monthly among them.

But the paper that would become the dominant news source for Columbia's first quarter-century was that puny little free "shopper" that started on a dining room table.

Planning for communications

Communications is one of the thinner volumes in the many Green Books that document the meticulous planning and proposals for all aspects of Columbia life.

"The whole subject of communications in the planning of Columbia can only be described as a mystical religious icon which everybody revered with poignant regularity," wrote Wallace Hamilton, Rouse's director of institutional planning. "'We've got to think about communications,' people would say. But nobody ever really did anything about it, except write long reports for longer conferences and got more and more people into the act to share the general confusion."

"We got intrigued with technology for technology's sake and lost track of function," Hamilton observed.

Although their focus was on technology, the goal of the planners remained the same as for the village centers and neighborhood gathering places—encouraging community life and spirit. The early planners reached out to the companies that were developing futuristic technologies that would become the driving forces of American communications in the final decades of the 20th century—cable TV and then the Internet. But the planners were 10, 20, even 30 years early as they contemplated interactive TV loops and other forms of electronic two-way communications.

For those under 40 and those who have forgotten, it's worth refreshing what communications was like in the 1960s.

There were telephones, an invention of the late 19th century, but they were all what we now call "landlines," connected by copper wires, owned and operated by a single local monopoly we called "the telephone company."

There were urban TV stations, most of them part of the three major networks, that broadcast over the airwaves to antennas. And radio, the early 20th century invention, was available almost everywhere.

All these systems were regulated by the government at the federal or state level, with a complicated set of licensing.

Some of the planners at the Rouse Co. wanted its own radio station, but that didn't happen until WLMD, a Laurel station, set up a small studio in the mall in 1979. It lasted only a couple of years.

Columbia's central location in the Baltimore-Washington corridor put it at the edge of both these big media markets. The available television channels were used up, with only slim possibilities for a UHF TV channel and an AM radio station.

In October 1970, after much back and forth, Howard Research and Development, the Rouse division managing the new town, announced that Time-Life had been granted a franchise to establish cable television in Columbia. But the cable franchises were still under local control, and Time-Life backed out when it balked at provisions in the Howard County legislation. A local group won the rights in a partnership with Warner Communications. The Howard franchise was sold to Storer Cable, which became Comcast in 1993.

Local programming

Andy Barth moved to Columbia in August 1971, the week The Mall in Columbia opened, conveniently located between Baltimore where he worked as a reporter for WMAR TV (Channel 2) and his wife's job in Silver Spring.

"At first it was just convenient; then we became converts" to the Columbia vision of an integrated, inclusive community, said Barth, now press secretary to Howard County Executive Allan Kittleman.

For two or three years, WMAR had a bureau located in the Exhibit Center next to Lake Kittamaqundi staffed by reporter Glenn Cox.

"TV was very, very competitive then," said Barth. He eventually spent 35 years at WMAR before retiring to run for Congress in 2006.

"Columbia was a story at that point" as the new town grew, he said. "We did a birthday story pretty much every year."

Many Baltimore TV personalities made Columbia their home, recalled Barth: the late Al Sanders, Denise Koch, Dick Gelfman, Jeff Hager, and briefly, a young Oprah Winfrey, among others.

Throughout the years, Howard County and Columbia have been part of a tug of war for eyeballs between rival TV stations for this lucrative, high-income market.

There were many TV stories about the progressive ideas embodied in the Columbia concept, such as interfaith religious centers, but "at some point it stopped being new," said Barth.

Yet, for all that, these were stories done for a wider regional audience.

In its first 30 years, the Columbia community relied on the oldest of the mass media, newspapers, and for several decades that medium was the Columbia Flier, from its start delivered free to all the households in town.

The Flier

Two years after Columbia Life folded, and two non-journalism jobs later, a position finally opened at the Columbia Flier, where I had done some freelance writing. I had already helped the Flier move from its small flexi size into the tabloid it became in 1974, growing to 64 pages. After I became associate editor in 1975, I covered education, business and politics. In 1976, I wrote the cover story for its first 100-page issue, a piece titled "Banned Books" on efforts to ban some books from school libraries.

We now know that we were all working in the heyday of the newspaper industry—not just in Columbia or Maryland, but in the United States. Advertising revenues were bulging, profits were ballooning, staffing soared at every publication.

The Patuxent Publishing staff, including the Columbia Flier, in the foyer of the Flier building sometime in the 1980s. In the lower center are Publisher Zeke Orlinsky (mustache, sweater) and General Manager Jean Moon. Editor Tom Graham is at the very bottom right; Len Lazarick is second person to his left. Photographer unknown.

There were people who loved the Flier; there were people who hated the Flier, particularly the liberal bent of its publisher Zeke Orlinsky and his weekly "Publisher's Note." But love it or hate it, people read it. At one point, a survey found that 92% of Columbians read the paper that landed free every Thursday on their doorsteps and driveways.

This was not your traditional newspaper produced by traditional newspaper people. Its models were magazines and the alternative city papers that grew out of the '60s counterculture. Its editors didn't just read the Washington Post and the New York Times, but the New Yorker and the Village Voice. It was in sharp contrast to its stodgy competitors, like the Sun.

The Flier's sketchy origins in 1969 certainly gave no hint of the powerhouse it would become.

"I got pissed at something in the Howard County Times," recalled Orlinsky in a recent interview from his home in Westport, Conn. "I didn't have a vision."

The first issue of the Flier was indeed a flyer—eight pages of legal paper folded with a Merriweather Post Pavilion ad on the front, ads for cars and tires, and a calendar of events. This first issue on Columbia's June birthday in 1969 was reprinted several times over the years as a reminder of how far the newspaper had come.

When Jean Moon joined the fledgling operation as a writer two years later, free circulation had grown to 9,000, and there was real news in the Flier, but they were still cutting and pasting the typewritten copy on a dining room table.

At the time, Orlinsky wrote: "To reflect the growth of a new city like Columbia is to meet new challenges. It calls on a publisher to throw away the old and tired concept of journalism. Journalism is more than just information and news. Journalism should excite and guide a community."

That statement was still being pointed to 20 years later in a history of the paper given to new staff members of a much larger enterprise.

Moon, who had come to Columbia with her husband Bob for his job as an architect at the Rouse Co., was totally on board with the concept of community journalism—"that we weren't dailies" and the mission was to "play a role in the community," she recalled in an interview.

By 1973, Moon was editor and general manager, she had hired Graham, and the staff had grown several times. By the time I joined the staff on July 31, 1975, it was operating out of a building on Route 108. It moved again to Wilde Lake Village Center, and in spring of 1978, we moved into the Flier building on Little Patuxent Parkway, an unusual building designed by Bob Moon, standing out amid the town's bland architecture, with its white metal sides and sloping fronts of glass.

There were no crusty old editors looking over our shoulders, telling us "we don't do that here." Jean and Zeke—and we often talked about them that way in this family-like operation—were still in their 30s; Tom and I were in our 20s, and the staff was of similar age. While Tom and I did take photos, we eventually brought on a staff of talented photographers who made that a hallmark of the paper in future years.

The Flier was more than just a writers' paper. What's striking going through boxes of old clips I dragged out for this book was how closely we covered this new community—the opening of restaurants, the closing of stores, the community dustups, the arguments over tot lots and door colors, the nitty-gritty of everyday life. While there were wonderful photo spreads and long features, there was also column after column of "notices" about routine events and meetings.

Because of Jean Moon's proclivities, there was massive coverage of the performing arts, not just in Columbia (Merriweather Post Pavilion was going strong as a venue for big acts), but in Washington and Baltimore too.

There was local sports galore including the long-time weekly column by Stan Ber called "Bits and Pieces," a column that predated my arrival and survived long after I left 21 years later. Stan, like many of the other writers, was community-bred. His day job was at the National Security Agency where he did what can never be disclosed and where they answered the phones cryptically with the last four digits of the extension you called.

Most of us lived in Columbia. We were part of the community, and the community was part of the paper. Page three had the signed "Publisher's Note"—none of this unsigned editorial page stuff of the old school—and then there were the letters, so many letters from Columbians, often complaining about Zeke's emotional diatribes or other coverage that pushed the envelope, like the time we put the full-page image of a mammogram on the cover to illustrate a story on breast cancer.

The Flier was the way the community talked to itself, understood itself, remembered itself.

The advertising flowed in—all the newspaper staples—cars, groceries, real estate, classifieds. "The smartest thing was not selling ads by the inch," as dailies did, producing those odd-shaped page wells, Orlinsky said. The Flier sold eighth-, quarter- and half-pages that made design easier and more attractive.

More advertising meant more money, more pages, more stories to fill them, more staff to write and illustrate them, and more listings—and made it a more attractive target for acquisition.

The sale of the Flier

The night of Nov. 7, 1978, a major gubernatorial election, I was covering the returns in the Kiwanis Hall in Ellicott City, and a reporter from the Howard County Times asked me my reaction to the sale of the Columbia Flier.

I was floored. Sale, what sale? Jean had tried to have me tracked down that night—this was decades before cell phones—so I would not learn of the deal from our local competitors who had gotten wind of it.

Who were these guys at Whitney Communications? Turns out these guys—and yes, they were all guys—were some of the classiest in the business. The chairman, Walter Thayer, had been the publisher of the vaunted New York Herald Tribune, and the president was John Prescott, former president of the Washington Post Co. Millionaire John Hay Whitney had founded the company.

It was one of the best things that ever happened to us. Jean and Zeke were left fully in charge. A year later we bought the Howard

County Times and other papers in the chain. I got to spend full-time in Annapolis during the 90-day sessions as political editor. When John Hay Whitney died in 1982, the partners created a working fellowship that sent Tom Graham and then me to Paris for a year at the International Herald Tribune, where Whitney had been the managing partner of a three-way ownership split with the Post and The New York Times.

We won award after award, both state and national, for writing in many categories, photography and design.

The Flier kept chugging along, and in 1988, our newspaper group, now called Patuxent Publishing, bought Times Publishing in Towson and its five newspapers, including the Towson Times and the Jeffersonian. I became managing editor of seven Baltimore County papers.

"We never recovered from that purchase," said Jean Moon in a 2016 conversation. In hindsight, she said, "We overpaid for those newspapers" and struggled to make them generate enough return on that investment.

Management began making cuts in the 1990s as Maryland experienced a harsher recession than the rest of the country. In 1995, a Whitney Communications partner and Zeke told Jean Moon she needed to go, and in June 1997, six months after I left, Patuxent and the Flier were sold to the Baltimore Sun and its new owner, Times-Mirror.

"I really don't think [the sale] will change anything" about the newspapers, Orlinsky told me for a story I wrote about the sale in the Business Monthly. "It's not in their interest to screw it up."

Orlinsky stayed on as a consultant for a year, having twice sold the same paper at a handsome profit. He was wrong about nothing changing.

Orlinsky says now he had seen some of the handwriting on the wall a few years before as the Internet began to spread. "I didn't understand it" but "I knew that it was only a period of time [before] newspapers would lose those categories" of classifieds—employment ads, real estate and cars.

What began as small dips in revenue in the 1990s became a steady downhill slide and then, in 2008, as the Great Recession hit, newspaper revenues fell off the cliff. As advertising evaporated, pages and coverage were cut, as were the reporters and editors who produced them.

Along the way, Times-Mirror sold the Sun and the local papers to the Tribune Co., which went private and then bankrupt for years, and now has the god-awful name of "tronc." Over the years it has decimated staff and closed offices, including the Flier building on Little Patuxent Parkway in 2011.

The Flier is now run by editors in the Sun's downtown Baltimore building. What were once several independent news operations in the city and the five counties that surround it are now under one owner, the Baltimore Sun Media Group, with copy shared among all. In the Flier you can read articles you may already have already read in the Sun, or the other way around.

The only locally owned and operated news outlet is the Business Monthly, where these chapters first ran as a series. Started in February 1993 by Ed and Carole Pickett as the Columbia Business Journal, it was geared to just a sliver of the community. It became the Business Monthly nine months later after Orlinsky registered all the other likely publication names, and the Picketts decided not to fight him.

Carole grew up as Carole Ashbaugh in western Howard County, married Ed and had three children at a very young age. By the time they returned to Howard County, they had run several newspapers in Vermont, and radio stations as well.

Carole, now Carole Ross, says it was her idea to start a business paper here, with Ed as editor. When Ed soon after decided also to launch the Columbia Daily Tribune, that was the last straw for Carole after many, many straws with her spendthrift hubby.

She called it quits on the marriage, but kept the Business Monthly, $68,000 in debts and all. But aside from Ed's spending, "It made money from the very first issue," she said.

From its start, one of the Business Monthly's gems were the columns by Dennis Lane, ostensibly about his field of commercial real estate, but really wise and funny commentaries on public life. Under the moniker WordBones, he became one of the first, best and most provocative bloggers on local life and added a podcast with attorney Paul Skalny to his media chops until he was brutally murdered in 2013. On Oct. 19, 2016, a new road near Merriweather Post Pavilion, where Dennis worked as a teenager, was dedicated as part of Columbia's revitalized downtown. It is called Dennis Lane in an amusing tribute to an amusing writer in a town full of weird street names drawn from poetry and unconnected to persons living or dead.

Carole sold the Business Monthly in 2002 to Becky Mangus and Cathy Yost. I worked with both sets of publishers from 1998 to 2006, when I became State House bureau chief of the Baltimore Examiner, which covered Howard County in its typically haphazard way, with its usually erratic free delivery, until its untimely demise in 2009.

From left: Carole Pickett Ross, former publisher of the Business Monthly; the late Maggie Brown, president of the Columbia Association; and the late Judy Tripp, editor of the Business Monthly. Business Monthly photo.

Not the only game in town

The Flier was never the only game in town. The Sun had an Ellicott City bureau for many years with Mike Clark reporting there for decades; the News-American and Evening Sun were represented too.

In the early 1980s, attempting to capture more suburban readers across the Baltimore region, the Sun set up the Howard Sun with a separate, and lower paid, staff that competed strongly with the Flier for stories and advertising. The Sun tried various configurations of separate Howard County sections for years after it bought the Flier and Howard County Times, and still has a thin section in the Sunday paper, though the content is often shared.

The Washington Post also had the Howard Weekly, part of a plan to open bureaus in all the counties it served. It leased premium space in downtown Columbia, but never filled it. It was later replaced by the Howard Extra. The Post, for which I worked part-time on the national copy desk for eight years, and for which Tom Graham has worked since 1999, has severely cut back local coverage under the ownership of Amazon's Jeff Bezos.

Many Columbia residents mourn the loss of the Flier they remember from years ago, a fat, thriving community newspaper operation. Jean Moon, who created a new career for herself as a public relations consultant to some of the biggest organizations in Columbia, said, "People complain all the time" about how thin the Flier is. But she said those are people of "our generation," meaning the over-65 crowd, bemoaning the good old days.

"I don't feel a concern about creating community anymore," Moon said. "People see no need for a community newspaper."

Pat Kennedy, now 82, president of the Columbia Association from 1972 to 1998, is one of those who mourns the loss of the Flier, which he saw as crucial in creating a vibrant community.

The building that housed that crucial community builder has sat empty for several years. Howard County Executive Ken Ulman wanted to turn it into a business incubator, but for the Kittleman administration, the price tag was too high. It may now be torn down and replaced with "affordable housing" as part of downtown Columbia's revitalization.

For Kennedy, the tearing down of the Flier building stands as "a metaphor for the decline of the newspaper industry" as a whole.

After this chapter initially appeared in print and on the web, I heard from Lowell Sunderland, who had edited a Columbia magazine for Rouse, then the Columbia Times in the 1970s, and later was editor of the Howard Sun. Said Sunderland:

"You have pegged the Flier exactly right. My only addition would be this: Jean and Tom's real talent, I still believe, was totally understanding the community 'vibe' of Columbia. Issue after issue, for years, the paper accurately and subtly caught and illuminated the life of the new town. They made the paper indispensable reading if you lived and, especially, if you were raising a family, in Columbia. The ad side of the paper had the same impact and inside knowledge of what Columbians wanted.

"Sadly, no more. None of that. In fact, news coverage of Columbia, and all of Howard County, for that matter, is pathetic from both the Baltimore and Washington dailies."

And there's no sign robust community coverage will return in print or electronically, despite abortive efforts.

The Columbia Flier building on Little Patuxent Parkway has sat vacant for several years and may be torn down. Photo by Len Lazarick.

The Howard County Council in 1978 on its old elevated dais. From left, Elizabeth Bobo, appointed in 1977, elected county executive in 1986, lost reelection bid in 1990, elected to the House of Delegates in 1994, retired in 2014; Lloyd Knowles, elected in 1974, lost a reelection bid by district to Ruth Keeton in 1986, now married to Liz Bobo; Ruth Keeton, elected in 1974, resigned from the council in 1989 due to her worsening Alzheimer's disease; Ginny Thomas, elected in 1974, elected to the House of Delegates in 1982, lost election for state Senate in 1994; and Thomas Yeager, elected in 1974, elected state senator in 1982, defeated for reelection in the Democratic primary by Ginny Thomas in 1994. Below them is council secretary Russell Sadler who was appointed a district court judge in 1980, and retired in 1996. Photo by Howard County government. Courtesy of Columbia Archives

Chapter 5:
Politics: The shifting weight of Columbia political power

As the election returns came in the night of Nov. 5, 1974, Howard County's old guard was riding high. It looked like their campaign to "Beat the BLOC VOTE" from Columbia had worked. Republicans would get their first county executive, and car dealer Charlie Miller, who had approved the plans to build Columbia as an elected county commissioner, would get to stay on the County Council.

But as the results from Columbia precincts poured in later, elation turned to shock. The new town had voted overwhelmingly for the liberal slate of Democratic candidates, nine to one. People who had lived in Howard County for just a few years beat the old timers.

Three of the five new County Council members actually lived in Columbia, and one, Dick Anderson, was even a former general manager of Howard Research and Development Corp., the Rouse Co. division building the planned community. A fourth, Lloyd Knowles, had moved near Columbia because of the new town, and the new county executive, County Council Member Ed Cochran, a mild-mannered research chemist at the Johns Hopkins Applied Physics Lab where Knowles also worked, was seen as liberal, too. Only Cochran was born or raised in Maryland.

The old guard's dire predictions of bloc voting may have been a campaign ploy to rile up their constituent base, but they also riled up the bulk of Columbians who had voted 8-1 for liberal Democrat George McGovern for president two years before. The rest of the county Democrats had voted in the primary for George Wallace, the segregationist who survived an assassination attempt in nearby Laurel the day before the primary.

"No to the backroom political takeover of Howard County by Columbia block voting," blared the ads in the Howard County Times. "No to the instant slums of public housing and poor construction....No to the social adventurism which has encouraged the attack on our way of life, fostered crime and looked favorably on negative lifestyles."

No need to read between the lines to feel the hostility to what were seen as core Columbia values—an economically and racially diverse community. These values of Jim Rouse's Columbia had attracted liberals from near and far, particularly its pledge of the racial integration uncommon in Maryland at the time. The schools in Howard County had been segregated until just 10 years before, and Cochran, serving on the school board, had helped desegregate them.

"The Republicans converted the campaign into a referendum issue of new versus old, which was very harmful," Cochran told the Baltimore Sun's Mike Clark after the election. He promised a more unified county government.

The election wasn't just about values; it was about sheer numbers. Because of Columbia, Howard County's population had grown from 50,000 to 100,000. The people outside of Columbia simply got outvoted.

Key decisions 10 years before

The biggest decisions that impacted that election were made 10 years before.

In 1962, Charlie Miller had been elected as a county commissioner on an anti-growth platform. Despite that, Rouse and company had persuaded him, the rest of the political establishment, and most importantly, their constituents, that a planned city of 100,000 was the best solution to the development pressure that was inevitable on a largely rural county between Baltimore and Washington suddenly accessible through the new interstate highways. The developers had spent months talking to any community group that would listen.

Attorney Jack Jones, who represented the Rouse Co. in many of the land deals, recalled in an interview with Rouse biographer Josh Olsen decades later: "So it was clear the development was going to come, and the question was do you want orderly development or do you want piecemeal and Levittowns?"

Two key points that had helped persuade the three commissioners who ran the county government and their constituents: Columbia was not going to be a burden on the county or raise their taxes. It would expand the commercial property tax base and be a net gain.

Rouse and the working group had long internal discussions about what form of government Columbia should have. At one point there were 12 different options on the table.

They included forming a municipality or special tax district; making the cost of community facilities part of the price of a house; going into partnership with the county government as the developer; and even the rather easily dismissed option of establishing a new county. At one point, they even discussed creating a separate school district just for Columbia, so that more money could be put into education.

All the options had drawbacks, principally political. The state legislature or the county commissioners would have to approve these new entities. Only Baltimore and Howard counties have none of the 153 municipalities in Maryland; Ellicott City, as its name implies, was once incorporated but dissolved in 1935.

The developer chose instead to continue to rely on the county and state for basic governmental services: for running the schools (after the developer gave them the land), for maintaining the roads (after the developer paid to have many of them built), for police and fire protection (still mainly provided by volunteers), and of course for the most important thing that the developer needed up front and would continue to need for a long period: zoning and control over what would be built where.

The Swiss-cheese problem

Most of the governmental options Rouse considered also had the Swiss-cheese problem. Columbia may have been 14,000 acres of mostly farmland, but there were holes in the cheese all over. These included residential developments such as Allview Estates, Guilford Downs and Sebring—"enclaves," the planners called them—and even ongoing farm operations, like Sewell's Orchard, and many smaller holes of one or several homes. These all came to be called "out-parcels."

Governmental entities depend on having contiguous land mass, not a Swiss cheese. They also aren't allowed to go into substantial debt without the tax base to support it.

Yet Rouse wanted to provide the new residents of Columbia with immediate amenities, like swimming pools, neighborhood and community centers and bike paths, through "pre-servicing." This involved substantial debt.

The eventual decision was to take the existing concept of a homeowners association, generally used for small developments, and scale it up beyond all recognition into a huge, multi-faceted organization to be known officially as the Columbia Park and Recreation Association, later shortened to Columbia Association, and generally compressed simply to CA.

This was not a governmental unit but a nonprofit community association that was established through perpetual covenants on the land and funded by a lien on every parcel of land in Columbia— essentially a property tax on residential and commercial real estate.

This would allow CA to go into debt, pre-servicing community and recreational facilities and financing them out of future revenues to be paid later on. This also kept the debt off the already debt-heavy books of Howard Research and Development Corp. This legal construct outside of government also could be controlled by the developer through its private board of directors.

"HRD felt that the ultimate fulfillment of the overall plan demanded a high degree of control over the new community during the 15-year development period," said Wallace Hamilton, Rouse's director of institutional planning, in a July 1964 memo.

But they also toyed with the problem of self-government and the advice from one member of the working group that "one of the requirements for a mentally healthy community was a sense of potency in the management of communal affairs."

At the same time, Jim Rouse, mindful of problems another developer had had in Illinois, "pointed out that political power needed to be held by the developer in considerable measure during the development period," Wallace explained. He quoted Rouse in a later session. "We're going to have to make some tyrannical decisions around here."

While the developer controlled CA through its board of directors until 1982, from the start it also added elected representatives from each village to serve on the board. Those elected representatives came to be called the Columbia Council. Now the CA board and the Columbia Council are basically one and the same, except the CA president also sits on the board.

Jim Rouse, left, presents a symbolic key to the Mall in Columbia to Howard County's first County Executive Omar Jones on Aug. 1, 1971.

Real political power

The real political power over the major institutions in Columbia and Howard County was at the county level. That's what Columbia Democrats grabbed in 1974.

In the early 1960s, Howard County might have been still largely rural and segregated, but it recognized that change and growth were coming. In 1965, voters mounted a successful petition drive to establish a charter commission to draft the county executive-county council form of government. This would replace the commissioners— governing by an elected three-member committee—and create a strong, elected executive with a county council as a legislature, giving local officials greater control over county laws. The elected commissioners were dependent on the legislature and the three-member county delegation to the State House for changes in local laws, as Carroll County still is today.

County voters approved the move to charter government in 1968, electing Omar Jones, former principal of Howard High School, as its first county executive. A conservative Democrat—a common type then, but now an endangered species—Jones would win reelection in 1970 to a four-year term and then endorse Republican Howard Crist to succeed him in 1974, rather than a "bleeding-heart liberal" like Cochran.

Miller had not expected the influx of progressives that landed on his doorstep. The hot issues of the day now seem quaint: whether Howard County should have its own consumer protection agency and financial disclosure for county officials, among them.

There was no question that the new county executive and council members in 1974 listened more closely to Columbia residents than the more unsympathetic executive and council members they succeeded. Further heightening the antipathy between the new and the old residents had been the competition over the county's first hospital. As initially conceived, the new Columbia Hospital would be open to only those who would also join the Columbia Medical Plan, a new-fangled health maintenance organization. Miller had backed the more traditional proposal from Lutheran Hospital to be built on his family's Gray Rock Farm.

Jim Clark

On a Sunday afternoon in August 1975, a few weeks after I joined the Columbia Flier, I was standing in the backyard of a townhome near Lake Kittamaqundi taking notes as a former governor of Georgia—a peanut farmer, no less—told a small crowd about his improbable run for president.

Jimmy Carter had just come from a private confab with some Washington journalists, including George Will, at the nearby farm of Sen. James Clark, Jr., one of Carter's earliest supporters.

Come January 1976, I would visit the

Maryland State House in Annapolis for the first time and get to know Jim Clark, probably the most important politician in Howard County at the time, aside from the county executive. He was a news source, he would become my political mentor and gradually, without me knowing it, he became my friend. (Clark's portrait, above, hangs with those of other Maryland Senate presidents in the James Senate Office Building Lobby in Annapolis.)

As a novice political reporter with a tiny, three-member county delegation to cover, I was fortunate that one of them was Clark. He was chairman of the Senate Finance Committee; he was state chairman of the campaign for the man who would become the next president of the United States, pitting Clark against Gov. Marvin Mandel and other machine pols; and in 1978, when his old state Senate chum Harry Hughes became governor, against all odds and the opposition of the Democratic Party establishment, Clark would become president of the

Maryland Senate, then, as now, one of the three most powerful posts in the state.

It probably did Howard County less good than it might have if a more conniving politician had the job. He was considered weak by many of his peers, especially compared to the new, ambitious speaker of the House, Ben Cardin, then in his mid-30s.

Son of a banker and Circuit Court judge, Clark traced his roots to the Clarks of Clarksville, and on his mother's side to the Ellicotts and relatives of Johns Hopkins.

Clark was a fiscal conservative, champion of the balanced budget amendment to the U.S. Constitution, but a progressive on other issues, including civil rights and the environment. Clark and his Senate ally, William James, crafted Maryland's open space program, and Clark pioneered the farmland preservation program into which he placed his own farm.

When Jim Rouse approached Clark to tell him about the plans for Columbia to be developed just across Route 108 from his farm, Clark asked but two questions: "First, is this city going to be open to everyone, and second, can you do this without driving our taxes through the roof?"

Clark was no foe of Columbia, but he and his political allies were hardly as liberal as the county officials Columbia voters catapulted into office in 1974. In the next election, Clark backed former Del. J. Hugh Nichols, then a state budget official, against Cochran, who was damaged by a controversy over the placement of a landfill.

J. Hugh Nichols

Born poor in Alabama, Nichols came to Howard County in 1957 to work for the National Security Agency in information systems. He took part in the petition drive for a Howard County charter, served on the charter commission and got elected to its first County Council when that charter passed in 1968. He was elected to the House of Delegates in 1970 after being appointed to fill a vacancy, and quickly became an appropriations subcommittee chairman. He was smart, ambitious and conservative, and willingly taught a novice

State House reporter like myself about the budget and General Assembly process.

Nichols easily beat Cochran in the Democratic primary for county executive by more than 3,200 votes, getting 57% of the Democratic vote, and handily won the general election. Living in the Sebring neighborhood, he was surrounded by Columbia but he was not of Columbia. He represented a brake on the more liberal members of the County Council.

Pat Kennedy, who served as president of the Columbia Association for more than 26 years, recalls that he had good relations with Cochran, but "Nichols had no interest" in helping with Columbia's more urban needs, such as the bus system it was running. "He was paying attention to his base," Kennedy said.

Nichols easily won re-election in 1982, but his career derailed at the end of his second term as he explored a run for governor as a Republican, switching parties in 1985. Facing the prospect of running against Democrat William Donald Schaefer, the popular Baltimore mayor, Nichols had trouble raising money and abandoned his quest for higher office.

He also abandoned Howard County five months before his term was up, resigning in July 1986 to take an economic development job with Middle South Utilities in New Orleans. The county's chief administrative officer, William Ned Eakle, served out Nichols' term. Nichols died in 2015 in Alabama.

Liz Bobo, Vernon Gray, Bob Kittleman

Nichols' successor couldn't have been more different. Liz Bobo was the first woman county executive in Maryland, and part of the liberal contingent on the County Council that had battled Nichols over the years.

Bobo, a Columbia Hills resident, had managed the campaign for the council slate that won in 1974. Then just 30, she was a young mother who had grown up in Baltimore. "I was painfully shy," said Bobo, as hard as that may be to believe for those who know her now.

Howard County Council member Elizabeth Bobo, left; Florence Bain, chair of the county's Commission on Aging; and County Executive J. Hugh Nichols break ground for the senior center in Harper's Choice that was eventually named for Bain. Her son Henry Bain was the consultant on government affairs to the Rouse Co. as it was planning the early stages of Columbia. Photo courtesy of the Columbia Archives.

She remembers sitting in the corner of meetings in Columbia with other young moms. other young moms. "The climate [Rouse] created here had a huge impact on me."

Cochran would appoint Bobo to the Board of Appeals in 1976, and then in 1977 she was appointed to the County Council for the seat left vacant when Dick Anderson left town for another job. Bobo's appointment also meant that a county that may have never had a woman hold any elected office before 1974 would have a majority of women on the County Council: Bobo, Ruth Keeton and Ginny Thomas.

In 1982, the county, whose population had been one-third slave when it was lopped off from Anne Arundel County in 1851, would get its first black elected official.

C. Vernon Gray, a Columbia resident and political science professor at Morgan State University, joined the council as part of a ticket that included Bobo, Keeton and Lloyd Knowles. Gray had been active in black political organizations, a Jimmy Carter delegate to the 1976 Democratic National Convention, and a governor's appointee to the state redistricting advisory committee. He would be a fixture on the County Council for 20 years, and came to be seen as a moderate, pro-business, pro-development swing vote on the council. It was his long tenure that led to the successful push for a charter amendment limiting council members to three four-year terms.

Gray, who grew up in segregated Calvert County, was a master of insider politics, and in the 1990s gained statewide and national recognition as president first of the Maryland Association of Counties and then of the National Association of Counties.

Joining Gray on the political stage in 1982 was another figure who would stick around for decades and lead the resurgence of the Republican Party in both the county and the state. Taking advantage of Howard County's doubled representation in Annapolis as its population ballooned, Bob Kittleman, a Westinghouse engineer who grew up in Iowa, became the first Republican Howard County ever sent to the state legislature.

Kittleman was not your typical Republican. Tall, lean and soft-spoken with libertarian leanings, Bob Kittleman had been active in the 1960s civil rights movement, participated in demonstrations to desegregate restaurants here, and became president of the county branch of the NAACP. His son Allan, who would follow his father's lead into politics, recalled the many black visitors to the family's Allview Estates home, making the neighbors nervous.

Even as a child, Allan Kittleman was politically aware, accompanying his father to political events. He recalled the "wild party" celebrating his father's election victory at the Chatham Lounge on Route 40 on Nov. 2, 1982, even though the GOP had elected but one candidate out of many on the ballot.

Bob Kittleman, who had lost a run for County Council in 1978, would serve in the Maryland General Assembly for another 22 years. He would become House minority whip and help to grow the GOP statewide from a small band of 17 members of the House of Delegates (12%) to 43 in 2003 (30%), picking up seats once held by conservative Democrats.

Pushing for council districts, targeting Bobo

The continued dominance of the council by Columbia Democrats sparked a movement to elect the five members by district, rather than at large. After two failed attempts, a bipartisan effort to amend the charter passed easily with 58% of the vote in 1984, despite the opposition of some council members and the political establishment.

Election by councilmanic districts allowed Charlie Feaga, who had led the effort, to win a seat on the council in 1986 after two failed attempts. Feaga was a native countian, longtime dairy farmer and conservative stalwart of the Republican Party.

The new district lines had also put Democratic council veterans Ruth Keeton and Lloyd Knowles in the same West Columbia district. Knowles lost. Gray was reelected in what would become the "black" district, and Angela Beltram and Shane Pendergrass, two citizen activists, were added to the council. Pendergrass, an artist and art teacher by training, would wind up serving two terms, and 22 years later, in 2017, is in her sixth four-year term in the House of Delegates, where she chairs the health committee.

Bobo's tenure as county executive was rocky, stirring intense opposition among business and development interests for her slow growth policies outside Columbia, insisting on protecting the environment and making sure the infrastructure could support new development. There was soon a target on her back.

One-time Columbia resident Joan Athen, former chair of the Howard County Chamber of Commerce and an elected official of the local and state GOP, remembered a group of people who met regularly "to get rid of Bobo" because of her opposition to the building of Route 100 and her perceived anti-development, anti-business posture.

The anti-Bobo group recognized that, to replace Bobo, they had to have "somebody who would be acceptable by a broad group of people," Athen said.

They settled on Chuck Ecker, the former deputy superintendent of schools, who had left the system in June 1989. Athen recalled it took "many more than one meeting" to persuade Ecker, then 61 and a registered Democrat, to switch parties and make his first stab at politics and run against an incumbent Democratic county executive.

Affable and low-key, Ecker had grown up on a farm in Carroll County and lived in the Beaverbrook section next to Columbia. He had spent his entire career in public schools and was hardly what voters might think of as a politico.

I had met Ecker first covering the Howard County school board in 1975, and in the spring of 1990, Athen, who had been a friend since her unsuccessful race for delegate in 1978, asked me to discuss press relations for a candidate training session. (At the time, I was managing editor of Patuxent Publishing's eight Baltimore County community newspapers and had no role in Howard County coverage.)

I wound up sitting next to Ecker at lunch that day, and he asked me what I thought his prospects were against Bobo. Relying on the conventional wisdom I still believe, in general, I told him that a campaign against an incumbent Democratic county executive, who I still thought was relatively popular, would be very difficult to win.

Ecker had the backing of developers and other business interests, and ran some masterful ads against Bobo. But "the night of the election, it wasn't looking good," Athen recalled. She had promised Ecker that if he lost, she would help him raise the $30,000 he had loaned his campaign.

"It was scary," Athen said. The election was a squeaker. On election night, Ecker had won by only 244 votes. When absentee votes were counted, he had beaten Bobo by 450 votes, fewer than 1% of the ballots cast. In subsequent years, when I would run into Ecker, he would remind me of my gloomy forecast of his chances. If 226 people had switched sides, it would have been true.

From left: Howard County Executives Chuck Ecker (1990-98), Jim Robey (1998-2006), Ken Ulman (2006-14), and Allan Kittleman (2014-)

"I told people in my campaign that I was in trouble," Bobo said in a 2016 interview. "And they didn't believe me."

Across Maryland that year there had been a taxpayer revolt over rising property taxes. Voters kicked out four incumbent county executives, including Bobo.

"I loved doing that job," Bobo said, recalling some of its high points, like achieving a triple-A bond rating for the county. The loss was "painful," but "it's one heck of a learning experience."

One silver lining was her marriage to Lloyd Knowles. She believes that was unlikely to have happened if she had stayed focused on her career.

Despite the loss, her career was not over. Four years later, she was elected to the state House of Delegates in the west Columbia single-member district, serving there for 20 years. She fully embraced the "liberal" label and voted so independently at the State House that she never became part of the House leadership, as Shane Pendergrass eventually did.

Republican decade

Ecker, a fiscal conservative but one of the least partisan people imaginable, ushered in what would have to be called the Republican decade in Howard County.

Ecker's personal penchant for fiscal austerity was a useful tool in the early 1990s. The post-Cold War recession hit worse in Maryland than in other states and slowed revenue growth. Ecker instituted the $125 yearly trash collection fee, and he wound up being stingier with the school system than expected.

But the recession did not slow the growth. Howard County's population grew by almost a third (32%) from 1990 to 2000, increasing from 187,000 to 247,000, while the state's population grew by slightly under 11%. With growth slowing in Columbia, most of the new residents lived outside the planned community.

In 1994, a third Republican was elected to the County Council, Dennis Schrader, giving the GOP a majority on the county's governing board for the first time in 30 years, along with Ecker, the Republican executive. Republican Del. Marty Madden won a senate seat over Del. Ginny Thomas. More than half the state legislators representing the booming county were Republicans, including two of three senators.

"In 12 years, we went from zero to control of the government," observed Allan Kittleman.

Some Republicans became victims of their party's local success. At the time, Allan Kittleman, who was chair of the county GOP, warned, "We're going to start having [contested] primaries."

When Charlie Feaga ran for council in 1982 and lost, he was the lone Republican seeking one of the five seats. In 1998, he ran for executive and faced a serious primary challenge from his seatmate Dennis Schrader, a Columbian and relative newcomer to the county who was a vice president of the University of Maryland hospital in Baltimore.

Schrader depicted himself as a slower growth advocate and won the Republican primary with 52% of the vote. Many of Feaga's supporters felt that the farmer's decades of work for the GOP should have been rewarded, and Schrader should have waited his turn.

In the 1980s, "we were more united because we were small," said Allan Kittleman. Kittleman himself ran for County Council in Feaga's western Howard District, running in the primary against fellow Republican Gail Bates, a special assistant to Ecker and former manager of Feaga's campaigns.

Governing bureaucrats

While there was infighting among Republicans, Democrats took a page from the Republican playbook, recruiting former Police Chief James Robey to run for executive.

Robey was much like Ecker, who had appointed him as chief. He was a career public servant, rising 30 years through the ranks of the police force after his graduation from Howard High School. He had never been involved in partisan politics, but had vast local government experience as a high-level police manager. He was as much a Howard County native as Feaga, lived in Ellicott City, and his law enforcement credentials played well with Republican voters.

Despite spending less money, Robey easily beat Schrader, running strongly in Columbia and well outside it. With the election of Democrat Guy Guzzone to Schrader's southeast Howard County seat, the Howard County Council had three Columbia Democrats again. After just four years of GOP ascendancy, Democrats were back in control of county government.

Robey would keep the bureaucrats he had long worked with as part of the Ecker administration, running the government in a solid way without flair.

Gerrymandering—drawing legislative district lines for partisan advantage—is as old as the Republic, but it became more heavy-handed across the country in the 21st century. In 2001 in Howard County, with the Democratic council majority in charge of drawing the lines and a Democratic executive, they pretty much guaranteed that a liberal Columbia—then about two-fifths of the county—would dominate three-fifths of the five council seats, as it continues to do today, leaving a strong Republican district in western Howard County and a swing district in Ellicott City and Elkridge.

In earlier decades, Columbia made up perhaps half the county's population, but by the late 1990s, its proportion was on the decline and the issues were more partisan than geographic.

Despite its minimal high-rise density, Columbia is Howard County's urban core and center of commerce. It has more minorities and more subsidized and low-cost housing. From 1980 to 2000, Howard County's population more than doubled. For half these residents, Columbia was a fact of life when they arrived. Whether living in Columbia or outside it, people shopped at the mall or a village center; when in need, they went to Howard County General Hospital, where some of these new residents were born.

Born in Columbia

One of the new Columbia residents, born there in 1974, a year after the hospital opened, was the first child of Diana and Lou Ulman.

Ken Ulman grew up in the village of Dorsey's Search and attended Centennial High School, then the elite high school in the county. In hindsight, Ulman's rapid political trajectory seems clear.

He was part of student government at the University of Maryland, College Park, where he earned a bachelor's degree in government and politics. While a student, he interned at the White House and worked on President Bill Clinton's 1996 campaign and on Gov. Parris Glendening's 1998 re-election. He got a Georgetown law degree, and worked in Glendening's office as liaison to the Board of Public Works and secretary to the Cabinet.

When Mary Lorsung decided not to seek reelection to the County Council in 2002, he ran for her West Columbia seat. He was 28, and faced longtime Columbia resident Mary Kay Sigaty, then 52, in the Democratic primary. He campaigned doggedly through the hot summer, outspent her five to one—$50,000 to $10,000—and won by just 36 votes.

When fellow County Council Democrat Guy Guzzone decided not to run for executive four years later, Ulman took the plunge, running against Republican County Council Member Chris Merdon, an information technology professional who was just a few years older.

71

That year, Republican Gov. Bob Ehrlich, who had carried Howard County in 2002, lost his reelection bid to Baltimore Mayor Martin O'Malley, who won the county, as did Ulman.

At 32, Ulman became the youngest county executive in Maryland and the first Columbia native to hold the job. Four of the five County Council members were new, including his former foe, Mary Kay Sigaty, who took his council seat. An activist executive, he pushed a progressive agenda such as the county's own Healthy Howard health care plan and a downtown Columbia plan.

Advertising agency owner Roger Caplan, who had "really admired" Ecker and helped him get elected in 1990, pitched in for Democrat Ulman.

"Ken is one of the brightest guys I ever met," Caplan said in a 2016 interview. "He was exhilarating to work with," exploding with ideas. "He had the best political instincts."

Among them was keeping Robey's team of department heads, such as Dick Story, who served as head of the county Economic Development Authority for three executives. For Story, Ecker was the best. "He was sly; he was shrewd." But despite Ulman's youth and lack of business experience, he was a fast learner and quickly understood the needs of business. "He got it," Story said.

Sigaty saw him bring the values of Columbia to the executive office. "We have seen our county become a much kinder and gentler county," Sigaty told a Democratic dinner in 2013.

But like Nichols and Ecker before him, Ulman brought higher ambitions to his second term, exploring a race for governor earlier and with more persistence and fundraising know-how than either of them. When it became clear that Lt. Gov. Anthony Brown had the edge to succeed O'Malley, he joined Brown as his running mate for lieutenant governor.

That seemed a sure thing until along came Larry Hogan, with his running mate Boyd Rutherford, an experienced government executive and longtime Columbia resident. Despite Ulman's presence on the ticket, Hogan carried Howard County by 5,000 votes in 2014, twice the margin for Republican Allan Kittleman in his race for executive. Both major party candidates for lieutenant governor were lawyers who lived in Columbia.

"In any given year, it's a purple county," said Courtney Watson, the Democratic former County Council member who lost the county executive race to Kittleman. "It depends on how lethargic is the turnout for Democrats. All things being equal, it's a Democratic county."

Things are not equal for those rare times when a Republican runs well for governor, as Hogan did in 2014, and as did Del. Ellen Sauerbrey, who, although she lost her bid for governor, also carried Howard County by 5,000 votes in 1994. She lost to Glendening statewide by 6,000 votes.

Watson and Kittleman did not have quite the same Columbia bona fides as Ulman, but they came close. Both grew up near Columbia, and attended Atholton High School, surrounded by Columbia. They played in Columbia, they shopped in Columbia, and they shared many Columbia values.

"We were proud of Columbia," Watson said.

Kittleman is, of course, the son of Bob Kittleman, the one-time civil rights leader. He succeeded his father in the state Senate in 2004 when the elder Kittleman died. Watson's political pedigree is not as obvious. She grew up as Courtney Cochran, a daughter of Ed Cochran, the second county executive, elected with strong Columbia support.

The governing consensus

"I think Columbia has affected us in a very positive way," Kittleman said in a 2016 interview. Because of Columbia, "we are a more inclusive and open and tolerant community."

For evidence of this bipartisan community consensus, look no further than the autumn of 2016 and the swift reaction of the electeds of both parties condemning Democratic Sheriff Jim Fitzgerald. A report from the Howard County Office of Human Rights accused Fitzgerald of bullying and harassment of staff using racial and ethnic slurs. That is not who we are, said Republican Kittleman and his Democratic predecessors.

"People in Howard County want to see good government and not a lot of drama," Watson said. "Our citizens do not tolerate [drama] well." They believe in "making decisions for the common good."

Kittleman, who shares his father's libertarian streak, broke with his party on issues such as gay marriage, forcing him to give up his post as Senate minority leader. To get elected countywide, "you have to be more center right, you can't be far right," he said.

Yet the Kittleman-Watson contest also made clear the persistent split between Democratic Columbia and much of the rest of Howard County, particularly west of Route 29.

Watson carried most of the Columbia precincts easily, as well as many of the Ellicott City and Elkridge areas she represented on the council by smaller margins. Exclude Columbia precincts, and Kittleman would have won with a far greater majority than the 51 percent he got.

Another key part of the bipartisan community consensus is support for Howard County public schools, acknowledged as some of the best in Maryland and the country. The support is both moral and financial, from the best educated and most financially successful residents in Maryland and the country.

"Howard County has two key assets that set us apart from everywhere else," said Sigaty. "The school system and Merriweather Post Pavilion."

"The school system reflects the community," said Sigaty, a former teacher and school board member. "It is the absolute belief that it is the most important thing we do."

"The school system is what makes Howard County successful," said Watson, also a former school board member. "It's what leads Howard County's quality of life."

It's also what leads Howard County taxes to be higher than those in some nearby counties where less money is spent on schools.

As for Merriweather and the revitalization of downtown Columbia to create the high density urban core Jim Rouse envisioned 50 years ago, Kittleman has taken up the cause where Ulman left off.

He proposed tax increment financing (TIF), floating county bonds for downtown infrastructure based on the additional tax revenue the new buildings will bring. Many have called it a "developer handout," but Kittleman sees that as no more a handout than the original zoning the county gave the Rouse Co. for 14,000 acres of farmland.

"I'm glad Columbia never incorporated," said state Sen. Gail Bates. "There would have been much more divisiveness."

The Whole Food supermarket opened in August 2014 in the former Rouse Co. headquarters on Lake Kittamaqundi. There for a bread-breaking ceremony were, from left, Howard County Executive Ken Ulman, County Council members Courtney Watson and Mary Kay Sigaty; Del. Liz Bobo, the former Howard County executive; and Whole Foods Mid-Atlantic President Scott Allshouse. Ulman had worked hard to get a Whole Foods to Columbia. County government photo by Scott Kramer. Courtesy of Columbia Archives

The Harriet Tubman building was once the "colored" high school. Photo: Len Lazarick

Portraits of 63 years of Howard County public schools superintendents hang on a wall outside the board room at the school system's headquarters on Route 108. From right, they are: John Yingling (1949-1968); M. Thomas Goedeke (1968-1984); Michael Hickey (1984-2000); John O'Rourke (2000-2004); and Sydney Cousin (2004-2012). Photo: Len Lazarick

Chapter 6:
Education: Schools were crucial then and now

As I walked into the Harriet Tubman building in the fall of 1975 to cover my very first meeting of the Howard County Board of Education, it would be difficult to underestimate how little I knew about school boards or public schools or even the building I was entering.

In my 18 years of education, I had never attended a public school, if you don't count two night courses in accounting at Catonsville Community College.

As I made my way down what I recall as a rather dim corridor to what seemed like a converted classroom where the board met, I can't say whether I really had any notion of what the building had looked liked just 12 years before as Jim Rouse's company was beginning to purchase thousands of nearby acres that would become Columbia.

Back in 1963, the students walking through these same doors and down the corridor of this junior-senior high school were all "Negroes." No accident that the county's lone "Negro" high school was located on Freetown Road, one of the "colored" neighborhoods in rural Howard County where the freed folk lived.

That's the kind of school system Jim Rouse and his workgroup experts at Howard Research and Development, the development arm of the Rouse Co., spent days debating the following year as they planned every aspect of the new community as a "garden for growing people."

"Education was obviously a crucial element in the growth process," wrote Wallace Hamilton, Rouse's director of institutional planning, in a June 1964 memo. "But there was an additional reason for an intense interest in education." Rouse wanted to attract lots of research and development firms to the planned business parks.

"The employees in such industries were in general well and stably paid, well educated and good prospects for both housing and energetic community development," Hamilton wrote. "Such people took their own education seriously—and their children's education seriously."

"In the field of education, HRD's moral and economic ambitions coincided," he said.

Not fertile soil in a rural county

The Howard County school system was not exactly fertile soil. Ten years after the U.S. Supreme Court declared "separate but equal" schools unconstitutional, it was still in the process of desegregating. Overall, it ranked 15th in the state in per pupil spending, $380 a year; neighboring Montgomery County was the highest at $505.

HRD hired an education consultant, Christopher Jencks, who proposed a much more innovative and individualized approach to schooling. He had little faith in the current school board or its administrators.

The Jencks study was "the beginning irritant or stimulant for change in the school system," Mary Hovet, longtime assistant superintendent for curriculum, would write 30 years later.

Over the course of months, Jim Rouse, his team and consultants argued how to create a school system for the highly educated workforce they were hoping to attract. They mulled creation of a separate school district funded by extra taxes on the town's residents; they considered private schools or a mix of both. Ultimately they realized that this wasn't going to work—politically or practically.

At the same time, they found the administrators and the school board remarkably receptive to their ideas. The board "felt that the new town development could be used as a lever to raise the level of the entire county school system," wrote Hamilton. The five-person board, while appointed by the governor, was essentially hand-picked by Howard County's lone state senator, James Clark, Jr., who had chosen some progressive nominees, including the first black woman on the board.

The school system itself used a federal grant approved by the Maryland Department of Education to hire its own outside consultants to recommend a 10-year plan. With the tremendous growth expected from a blossoming Columbia, the two professors it hired proposed that schools be physically adaptable and autonomous, with principals and teachers allowed to experiment. They emphasized individualized instruction, team teaching, independent study and taking advantage of new technologies.

The board adopted their recommendations, leading to a proliferation of open space schools designed for team teaching, putting them on the cutting edge of what was a national trend.

A superintendent for the long term

To preside over this immense change and growth, in 1968 the board hired M. Thomas Goedeke (go-deh-KEY), a 29-year veteran of Baltimore City schools.

When he arrived, Howard County had 13,000 students in 21 schools. When this imposing man with a no-nonsense demeanor left 16 years later in 1984, the county had nearly twice as many students and 49 schools.

"It was a very exciting period," Fred Schoenbrodt told the Baltimore Sun for its January 2000 obituary of Goedeke.

Schoenbrodt, a political ally of Sen. Jim Clark, served on the Howard school board from 1962 to 1978, including 12 years as its president. "It was the beginning of Columbia, when the school system was pretty much rural. That's when we became a suburban system overnight." Schoenbrodt and Goedeke were partners for those first 10 years as Columbia got off the ground.

In 1967, John Yingling was in his 18th year as superintendent of Howard County schools, in which he had spent his entire career. The 1968 annual school system report dedicated to the "Yingling years" noted that, in 1949, some schools still had been one-to-four-room, wood-frame structures. For one of them, the Ellicott City Colored Elementary School, Yingling had an outdoor pump installed to make up for its lack of running water.

In 1967, with all those consultants looking over his shoulder and the Columbia influx coming, he and the board had finally finished desegregating the schools, putting blacks and whites together in the same classrooms. They had restructured the system from the old 6-3-3 model with junior and senior high schools, to the 5-3-4 grade model with three-year middle schools, adding half-day kindergarten on the front end.

What Yingling kicked off, Goedeke brought to a new level.

"He was responsible not only for building but also for staffing and seeing that they were operating and doing the jobs that they were supposed to do," Schoenbrodt said. "A system that doubles in size practically overnight, that takes a lot of doing."

Goedeke and Schoenbrodt, both of that firm but kind-hearted German stock that so reminded me of my mother's family, were my educators in the ways of the school system. My reporting likely reflected their establishment view, and I spent more time in the boardroom than I did in the schools. The action there centered, as it often does today, on budgets, teacher contracts and administrative policy.

School construction was always top of mind. Gov. Marvin Mandel's promise to pay for constructing all the new schools in Maryland was being overwhelmed by pent-up demand from suburban growth. From 1971 to 1975, the state approved $1.2 billion for school buildings—the equivalent of $5.4 billion in today's dollars. Goedeke and Schoenbrodt were stunned when they attended a Board of Public Works meeting in late 1975 and heard Mandel describe the state funding as a "five-year program."

Goedeke said at the time that his understanding was that the program would go on "forever and ever."

Goedeke and Schoenbrodt moved Howard County schools in new and exciting ways that were experimental, even faddish. Epitomizing that approach was Wilde Lake High School, Columbia's first high school, which represented exactly what the consultants were talking about.

New school for a new town

If Columbia was a radical departure from haphazard suburban sprawl, Wilde Lake High was a radical departure from the traditional high school, both physically and philosophically.

The original Wilde Lake Middle School, right center, and Wilde Lake High School above it were both configured in the round. Both have since been torn down and replaced, as has much of the village center on the left. Photo: Morton Tadder Courtesy Columbia Archives

The center of the interior of the school was a "donut," with the media center at its core. "Because the Media Center is the focus of Wilde Lake High School," a student handbook explained as the school was about to open in September 1971, "much of its program will be devoted to meeting individual requests for information—whether its form be book, visual, magazine, tape or television."

The students were expected to learn at their own pace, guided by teachers.

"It is the hope of the faculty that the curriculum and the related experiences will provide each of you with the inspiration and competence to discover who and what you are."

One of the guiding principles was "the knowledge that this school is committed to making failure obsolete."

In fact, failure was impossible, except with special permission for a rare course. There were only three grades: A, B or C. If students didn't master the minimum requirements of a course, they kept working till they did master the material enough to get them a C.

The grading system was so novel that principal John Jenkins sent a special letter home at Thanksgiving that first year explaining it. The setup of the curriculum was so extraordinary that the school also developed a letter to explain to college admissions offices how to decipher the student transcripts.

The contents page of the handbook ended with a famous quote from poet Robert Frost:

"Two roads diverged in a wood, and I —
I took the one less traveled by
And that has made all the difference."

The less traveled path

Some students thrived on this less traveled path through the thicket of high school adolescence; others got lost in the woods.

As an education student at the University of Maryland College Park, Eric Ebersole got his student teaching experience in math at Wilde Lake High, and joined the faculty there in 1980. He stayed for 22 years, teaching mathematics and computer science, then went on to head departments in newer high schools.

"There was something uniquely cool about Wilde Lake," said Ebersole, now a member of the House of Delegates whose District 12 includes Wilde Lake. "The kids there had a sort of open-mindedness. It was very refreshing to be around them."

Novelist Laura Lippman resurrected her 1970s high school experience in the sometimes dark novel "Wilde Lake," out last spring. In July, she reminisced more personally in the British Daily Mail:

"When I decided to write about my old high school in a novel, I realised there was much to admire. Yes, it was crazy to expect adolescents to make sound decisions about how to allocate their time. However, students who were motivated could soar at Wilde Lake. It was a great place to be an outlier. There were quite a few success stories, now that I began to take notice."

Lippman's Daily Mail piece—headlined with Brit hyperbole "My wild school days at Hippie High"—includes great photos of her time there, and even the photo spread about the school that ran in Life magazine, typical of the national attention Columbia and its institutions received in its first decade.

Successes or no, Wilde Lake itself, its design or its programs, was duplicated nowhere else in Howard County. By the late 1980s, it went to standard grading, and in 1994, just 23 years after it opened, it was torn down and replaced by a more traditional school—though interior windows gave its classrooms some open space feel, Ebersole said. The attached Jim Rouse Theatre for the Performing Arts was deliberately constructed as not only a school auditorium, but a community venue for arts production.

The plan vs. reality

Wilde Lake High was not a model for other high schools in Columbia or elsewhere, but the way the three levels of schools were planned in Columbia's first village was the pattern Rouse and HRD expected to be followed in future villages.

Schools were seen as essential building blocks of community. Each neighborhood would have an elementary school, with most of the children able to walk to school. The elementary schools would feed into a middle school located near the village center, and these children would then move on to the nearby high school, also in the village center.

That was the pattern followed again in Oakland Mills, the first village east of Route 29: Three neighborhoods, three elementary schools; an Oakland Mills Middle School; and next to it on a connected campus, Oakland Mills High School. OMHS opened in 1973, two years after Wilde Lake High, but with a more traditional building, though with an initial open space design.

In a similar time frame, the schools in the Village of Harper's Choice were opening. Harper's Choice Middle School opened in 1973, and then came ...

"Wait a minute, not so fast," said the school board.

Sue Buswell was appointed to the Howard County Board of Education in 1973 as it began transitioning to an elected board, running for the seat in 1976 and then for reelection in 1980 before getting elected to the House of Delegates in 1982.

In those 10 years, as enrollment was ballooning, "we were constantly redistricting," building 13 new schools and renovating 12 others, she recalled.

"Rouse was marketing the high schools" as part of the planned community, but he was not providing as much land as the school system wanted, she said. "We were not building two-story buildings," as Wilde Lake High was.

Buswell, who lived in Elkridge at the time, said, "We have a county-based school system, and we felt it was important that Columbia be part" of that system.

"It was important that schools be placed where we wanted them placed."

The Harper's Choice residents felt entitled, and so did the developer. This was the Columbia plan, after all.

Not factored into the plan was the growing resentment that Columbia was getting all the goodies. Residents outside the town "went to look at a Columbia school, and they felt, 'We're so deprived,'" Buswell said.

The next high school to be built was Hammond, near the King's Contrivance Village Center, serving that very disjointed village that stretched almost from Route 29 to beyond I-95. Then came Centennial on Centennial Lane, not a Harper's Choice high school.

The Village of Long Reach was a special case, with the old Howard High just across Route 108 from the Phelps Luck neighborhood. Originally opened in 1952, Howard has had four additions over the years, and five renovations. Long Reach didn't get its own high school till 1996, as its fourth neighborhood grew.

Not every neighborhood gets an elementary

An additional problem for the Columbia concept of school sites was that the neighborhoods were not always generating enough children to fill the schools that were built. This was a problem for

Longfellow, one of the earliest Columbia neighborhoods, but the school board chose to close Faulkner Ridge Elementary in Wilde Lake instead, turning it into a staff development center.

"Faulkner Ridge was an excellent school, a place for our kids to grow up," one parent who lived across from the school told the Washington Post in 1983. "All we want is for our neighborhood to have its own school. We thought that's what Columbia was about."

The competing goals of the developer and the school system were best symbolized by the sign that long advertised a potential school site in the Hopewell neighborhood of Owen Brown. The school system chose to renovate the nearby Guilford Elementary School instead; the sign is gone and golfers sometimes still use the grass-covered acres next to the Hopewell pool as a driving range.

On the other side of Owen Brown, my own daughters were able to walk to what was unique in the county—an elementary school (Dasher Green) housed in the same building as a middle school (Owen Brown).

I didn't spend much time in the classrooms, if parents were invited, back in the 1980s and '90s. I do vividly recall being unhappy with the Whole Language approach to teaching reading and writing. Phonics was abandoned, and correct spelling in writing assignments was considered a curb on expression. Because I wrote and edited words for a living, I was banned from touching homework assignments where I couldn't fix spelling, grammar or punctuation.

Goedeke leaves, Hickey enters

In 1984, with Goedeke retiring, the school board hired Michael Hickey.

In backgrounds, they were very different. Goedeke was a Baltimore native who had risen through the ranks as a teacher, vice principal, counselor, principal and central office administrator before becoming the No. 2 man in Baltimore City schools, accumulating a series of degrees over the years as many educators do.

Hickey was from Washington state and had spent just two years as an English teacher; got his bachelor's, master's and Ph.D. in quick succession from the University of Washington; became a deputy superintendent; then served as superintendent of St. Louis Park, a small school system outside of Minneapolis for eight years before Howard County hired him.

"I really listened to principals, and I had some good principals to listen to," said Hickey, explaining how he dealt with his lack of in-school experience.

Like Goedeke, Hickey was liked and respected and would stay as head of Howard County schools for 16 years, as other large, urbanizing systems saw faster turnover in the top job.

In a 2016 interview, Hickey's assessment was blunt. Goedeke had managed "the transition from a rural mudhole of a system. He deserves a lot more credit than he got."

In his first annual report, Hickey acknowledged the challenges. "Over time it seems as if the purpose of schools has become that of doing everything for everybody. The years of affluence have encouraged us to take on every societal task, tackle the ills of society, and even attempt to solve our national problems by the vehicle of the public schools."

While Howard County schools grew by leaps and bounds in the Goedeke years, the largest and fastest growth actually came under Hickey. In 1984, the year he came, enrollment stood at 24,252, with 41 schools; the year he left there were 44,525 students in 65 schools—20,000 more pupils in 24 more schools, adding an average of 1,250 students a year, a growth paced unmatched before his tenure or since.

In 1990, the new statewide report cards from the Maryland State Department of Education confirmed that the students in Howard County scored the best in the state, a status that would continue for years, with some back and forth between Howard and Montgomery counties.

The report card "confirms that Howard Countians are receiving good value for substantial investment in education," Hickey said in his annual report. The schools were spending about $6,000 per student.

Tight times

"Ironically, because of the national economic slump, both our state and county government find themselves in desperate financial straits," Hickey then reported. The post-Cold War recession was more severe in Maryland. For the first time in decades, the school system in 1991 experienced a real cut in revenues—not just a reduction in the proposed increase, as happens often. That year the system got almost $2 million less than the previous year despite the continuing growth, representing $270 less per pupil.

The stingy appropriations in these lean years led to the impression that Hickey was on the outs with County Executive Chuck Ecker, who had competed for the superintendent's job and had served as Hickey's deputy. But Hickey said, "Chuck and I always got along well. He never turned me down on capital funds," his request for buildings to cope with enrollment growth.

Hickey's tenure was almost cut in half in 1992, when it seemed to him the school board was not going to renew his contract. By his own account, he was offered the job as head of the Wake County schools in North Carolina, a district that includes the state capital Raleigh. Hickey said his wife had already picked out a house, and he was due to give the Wake County board an answer the next day when he got a call around midnight in their hotel room from the Howard County board. They really wanted him to stay.

He did.

This was also the beginning of the era of state-driven mandated testing for accountability, a process where Maryland and state Superintendent Nancy Grasmick had taken the lead. The state board instituted a series of statewide accountability tests, and Howard County students always performed well.

"Reforms come to us by way of mandates," said Hickey. "There's always much political pressure to use the results in the next election."

"I still tell people to this day that this was the best job I ever had," said Hickey, now 78, who retired in 2017 from an endowed professorship in educational leadership at Towson University.

O'Rourke replaces Hickey

Hickey was followed by John O'Rourke as superintendent.

Courtney Watson, later to serve two terms on the Howard County Council and then run for county executive, was elected to the school board in 2002. She recalled that O'Rourke, who had come from a much smaller system, was getting "mixed reviews," and she found "a lot of unrest" in the school system. When O'Rourke's contract came up for review in 2004, the board held a private meeting, and all five members voted against renewing his contract because "the superintendent was not a good fit," said Watson, who was board chair at the time.

When the board asked O'Rourke to leave, he refused to go until his contract expired in June. "It was a siege," said Watson, but eventually O'Rourke took a buyout.

The board chose the just-retired deputy superintendent Sydney Cousin to replace him on an interim basis, and then signed on Cousin for a full term. "He's really what the school system needed at the time," Watson said.

Quiet, amiable and a good listener, Cousin was a calming presence and steady hand, eventually serving two terms in a time of slowing growth.

Outside forces

Perhaps more important than the superintendent in the 21st century was the influence of outside forces. First, in 2001, Congress passed the No Child Left Behind Act, the most intrusive federal intervention in local schools in U.S. history. Then in 2002, the Maryland General Assembly passed the Bridge to Excellence in Public Schools legislation. It provided over the next decade a massive infusion of state dollars into public schools, resolving long-running court battles over the state's failure to adequately support public education as required by the state constitution.

With the increased state funding and federal rules came new accountability measures, performance standards, testing and requirements for five-year plans to meet the heightened standards.

In addition to the legislative mandates, the county's demographic mix was changing. Howard County, and particularly

Columbia, was becoming more ethnically diverse, largely due to the attraction of many parents to the reputation of its fine schools.

Federal requirements for annual yearly progress in every school, new accountability for how the increased state dollars were spent, and a more diverse student body put new emphasis on tests, scores and reports. Howard County continued to shine, but there was a stress on quantifying its stellar achievements. This led to more mandated standardized tests at every level, and increasing complaints that "teaching to the tests" and the amount of time for the tests themselves were cramping teaching and learning.

A few years ago, as the problems with No Child Left Behind became apparent across the nation, a push came for uniform national curriculum standards, known as Common Core. Developed with foundation support by education experts in collaboration with the National Governors Association and state superintendents, the new curriculum was not technically a federal initiative, but the U.S. Department of Education dangled federal dollars to encourage states to implement it. Maryland was an early adopter, and stayed true to the program, while conservative political pushback led other states to abandon what they saw as federal overreach.

The goal of the new curriculum, known in Maryland as College and Career Ready Standards, was more in-depth study into fewer topics, with major shifts in the math and English/language arts curriculum. The new curriculum also required developing a new set of nationally standardized tests, in which Maryland took the lead.

New superintendent and a vision

Into this constraining mix of strictures and tests, the Howard County Board of Education, now seven members large but still elected countywide, brought a new superintendent, the third in 12 years, after having just three chief executives in the previous 51 years. Renee Foose was the first woman to hold the job and had been deputy superintendent in Baltimore County, a principal in Montgomery County, a high school science teacher, and while she earned her education credentials, a Maryland state trooper.

Responding to all the external demands on the schools, Foose and the board produced a five-year Vision 2018 strategic plan that launched in 2013, a year after she arrived. It had four broad goals and "22 associated outcomes" and "103 strategies" to achieve them. Instead of the slim annual reports the school system had generated for decades, the three annual reports on Vision 2018 are thick, 106-page documents full of scores, charts, graphs and data-points on Howard County schools.

Foose's progress in implementing the plan, meeting its goals and closing the achievement gap led the board to offer her another four-year contract in 2016. But there was vocal community disenchantment with Foose and the board, reflected in the results of the 2016 election in which three incumbent board members seeking reelection lost their seats.

A state investigation, mandated by the legislature, of the board's information practices found it did not meet state standards. Legislative auditors issued a sharply critical audit of some of its financial practices, and the board chair responded with an unusually testy response.

There is little question, even among current board members, that the board itself was factionalized and dysfunctional. It came as no surprise that Foose didn't survive after the arrival of the three new board members.

But all this, and much of this entire essay, is a top-down institutional narrative with little relation to what happens day-to-day in 76 schools with 54,000 children and their 4,100 teachers. Teachers teach, and students mostly learn, and they learn about many more subjects in many more flexible ways than when Columbia started 50 years ago.

Perhaps the largest irony as we look at Columbia schools today is that the 1960s planners and consultants were concerned that the schools in Columbia needed to be a lot better than they were in the rest of the county at that time. In measurable ways, today they are worse.

As planned, Columbia has indeed become Howard County's urban core, economically and racially diverse. Along with other pockets in the Route 1 corridor, Columbia has the county's highest concentration of lower-income residents, living in aging (and thus lower-priced) apartments, condos and townhouses—but these "lower-middle-class" incomes are only in contrast to one of the top five highest median household incomes in the United States, the wealthiest nation on earth.

Demographics may not be destiny, but the schools in Columbia, depending on the housing mix, are generally 18–30% white, with high concentrations of African-Americans and growing numbers of Latinos. Columbia's first neighborhood school, Bryant Woods, is 58% African-American, 11% Latino, and a Title 1 school based on concentrations of low-income students—53% of the kids get free or reduced price lunches. Its standardized test scores are below county averages and even below state averages. There are fewer experienced teachers with advanced degrees.

Other Columbia schools have similar statistics. Foose and the school board had been trying to put more resources into these schools and close the achievement gap.

As County Council member Mary Kay Sigaty said in the last chapter: "Howard County has two key assets that set us apart from everywhere else: The school system and Merriweather Post Pavilion."

"I feel our fortunes rise and fall on the school system," Courtney Watson said.

In 2017, that system is in flux at the top and struggles at the bottom, but is still overall one of the key assets that distinguishes Columbia and Howard County. It was the planning for Columbia that pushed it toward those heights.

Lifelong learning

The previously published version of this chapter wasn't able to deal with two major education institutions important to both me and "the growth of people" in Columbia: Howard Community College and the county library system.

In the fall of 1975, I wrote a Columbia Flier cover story called "HCC: College of the common man." Besides its sexist headline, I vaguely recall it as a puff piece about a kind of higher education that I didn't know much about. Re-reading it now, it is actually a pretty balanced description of a good community college. Much of the article is as relevant today as it was 42 years ago.

The college then was crammed into one building, with two new buildings about to open. Credit and non-credit classes were offered at night in public schools around the county. HCC had only been operating about six years, although it was officially created in 1965.

The Rouse Co. planners showed significant forethought in allocating as much land as they did for the college, and for the hospital as well. Now the two campuses have almost merged, but it took some vision to see them developing that way decades ago. One early drawing placed the college near where the Rouse Co. headquarters (now Whole Foods) would eventually be located. That clearly would have eaten up precious downtown land where the central library branch and apartments now stand.

Fast-forward 42 years, and Howard Community College looks like a major academic institution with 10 buildings, two big parking garages and two satellite campuses. Walking the quad, it gives me special pleasure that some of its buildings, galleries and halls bear the names of college patrons, donors and leaders who I have personally known. These include state Sen. James Clark Jr., one of its most enthusiastic backers from the start; developer Patrick and Jill McCuan; Pete and Beth Horowitz; former college president Mary Ellen Duncan; Jim Rouse and the Rouse Co.; and the late Sen. Bob Kittleman.

Community colleges had a huge growth spurt across the United States in the 1960s. They get vast bipartisan political support because of their open admissions policies and their general emphasis on workforce training, teaching and learning, as opposed to research.

In the Flier in 1975, I wrote:

"What has not really changed from its conception, according to HCC's president Alfred J. Smith, Jr., is the founding idea—an idea of serving all community needs for education beyond high school." [The Smith Theatre, scene of many plays, performances and community meetings, is named in his honor.]

The original building at Howard Community College was renamed for Sen. Jim Clark. Photo: Len Lazarick.

" 'We'll sponsor anything' that someone asks for, Smith claims. 'That's what confounds people,' he says. But 'that's what a community college does.' "

The college has had only four presidents in its 60 years. That longevity has been one of its assets, along with a generally strong seven-member Board of Trustees, appointed by the governor on the advice of local state senators. In 1986 and 1987, I got to teach a semester course in state and local government, filling in for a professor I first got to know reporting on that 1975 cover story.

There were other colleges on the scene in Columbia's early years, among them Antioch College. Other universities offered classes in Columbia, including Johns Hopkins, where I took some management courses. Only Loyola University of Maryland and the University of Phoenix now have permanent locations here, along with Lincoln College of Technology, a vocational-technical school. Of course, major state and private colleges and universities are within easy driving distance.

On May 25, 2017, Howard Community College celebrated its 46th annual commencement, with more than 1,300 students receiving associate degrees or certificates in the past year, its largest graduating class to date. Here are some other key facts about HCC.

- 14,467 credit students enrolled in fiscal 2016
- 15,751 noncredit continuing education students enrolled
- 42% of all Howard County undergraduates attend HCC
- 24% of graduating seniors from Howard County high schools enrolled in fall 2016
- 5,750 noncredit students received customized business training
- The average age of credit students is 26
- 37% attend full-time; 63% attend part-time
- 37% are white; 29% black, African-American; 13% Asian; 11% Hispanic/Latino
- 104 different countries are represented in the student body
- There are 1,409 employees, and the student-to-faculty ratio is 19:1

Library of the year

The third component of education in Columbia and Howard County is the library system. In 1963, rural Howard County hired its first professional librarian, Marvin Thomas. He would serve as head of the county library system till 1996. Columbia's first library was in the Wilde Lake Village Center.

Blessed with an educated population that has demanded high services, the county over the years has had the highest per capita lending rate for library materials in Maryland and among the highest in the country. Like the community college and the public school system, the Howard County Library system has also had strong, consistent leadership and generous public financial support. There have been only three library directors since 1963. CEO Valerie Gross is leaving in August 2017 after a 16-year tenure that emphasized her vision of "Library=Education," a community-based educational institution supporting both the public schools and lifelong learning.

In 2013, the Library Journal named the Howard County system the national Library of the Year. The Central Branch in Columbia's downtown has now been renovated twice. A new Central Branch is envisioned as part of the plans for the new Merriweather District.

The newest building at Howard Community College is the Science, Engineering and Technology building, referred to as STEM. Photo: HCC

Above: The Columbia Hospital and Clinics as it looked when it opened. Photo: Courtesy Columbia Archives. Below, part of the Howard County General Hospital on its campus as it looks today. Photo: Len Lazarick

Chapter 7:
Health care: Planning for a healthy community—
an innovative HMO, a hospital fight and the quest for wellness

Jim Clark lay unconscious in a wheat field on his farm off of Route 108 on the morning of March 28, 1947. The 28-year-old wartime glider pilot had tripped while planting clover, and the drill the horses were pulling had knocked him out as they dragged him across the field.

"The disk had cut my face badly with one eye severely hurt ... my back had been cut badly by the stones in the soil. The steel wheel had run against my left arm and caused a large gash," the farmer who would become Maryland Senate president in 1979 recounted in his autobiography that I helped edit 20 years later.

A young farmhand eventually found Clark, his wife Lillian covered him with blankets as he began to go into shock, and she summoned a local physician. The doctor "knew immediately that I had to go to the hospital, so he put me in his car and took me to Montgomery County Hospital at Sandy Spring, where they gave me emergency care," Clark wrote.

It's hardly unusual for a rural county in Maryland or anywhere in the U.S. not to have a hospital. It would be another 26 years before Howard County would get its own, just two miles south of the Clark family farm. Lillian Clark would eventually serve on its board.

The opening of that hospital in 1973, first called the Columbia Hospital and Clinics, would be one of the most controversial aspects of Columbia's early years. Its creation was fraught with community tension, political discord and hostility among competing groups, creating ill-will outside of Columbia that would last for decades.

Planning for health care

Health care was another key element the original Columbia planners focused on in their 1964 work sessions. Unlike the schools, land use, water, sewer and political structure, for which the Rouse Co. planners turned to government institutions that already existed in Howard County, they would need to look beyond its borders for help.

In the early 1960s there was still a limited number of doctors in Howard County, and anyone needing inpatient care would go to Montgomery General Hospital in Olney or to Saint Agnes Hospital on the western edge of Baltimore. But a time of change in American health care was beginning that would continue to evolve for the next 50 years. Columbia was poised to explore novel options.

Paul Lemkau, a mental health expert from the Johns Hopkins School of Public Health, had been in Rouse's early planning group. At the urging of Jim Rouse, leaders at the Johns Hopkins Medical Institutions became interested in delivering health care to the new planned community that Rouse projected would have 100,000 people by the early 1980s.

But first they had to overcome the objections of their own medical staff, who feared that the relatively affluent residents of the new town would draw resources from their inner-city hospital, distract from its role in teaching and research, and not attract the best physicians.

The project gained enthusiastic support and, most importantly, financing from the Connecticut General Life Insurance Co., which had provided the money to buy the land and develop Columbia. Connecticut General was particularly interested in participating in a new trend in health care delivery, as Hopkins planned to develop a health maintenance organization, a prepaid group-practice of medicine that would emphasize prevention and easy access to health care over the more traditional fee-for-service model. In 1969, they launched the Columbia Medical Plan (CMP), which would last for three decades.

HMOs, as they were dubbed, were popping up all over the country, offering comprehensive care employing salaried physicians in a single facility. I had already been a member of the Harvard Community Health Plan when I lived and worked in Boston, and felt the CMP was another attractive feature about our move to Columbia in 1973— especially since the group was connected to another world-renowned medical school, Johns Hopkins.

As noted in earlier chapters, the 1973 Arab oil embargo and a recession accompanied by inflation and high interest rates had played havoc with the Rouse Co.'s economic model. Sales of housing and land in Columbia slowed, pushing the entire project toward bankruptcy.

Little did I know in 1973 that, just five years after it got started, the Columbia Medical Plan was falling short of its membership goals and financial plan. The problems were spelled out in detail in the New England Journal of Medicine by two Hopkins docs intimately involved with the planning and operation of CMP, Robert Heyssel and Henry Seidel.

"By 1974, Columbia was expected to have a population of 64,000, and the plan a membership of 32,000," the doctors wrote. "In fact, by mid-1976, Columbia's population was 40,000, and the plan's membership a bit in excess of 19,000."

"The population base was simply not large enough," they concluded.

Despite early losses— $1 million in just its first three years— the Columbia Medical Plan continued to grow as the population rose, though at a slower pace than originally projected. In 1982, CMP was acquired by Blue Cross Blue Shield of Maryland. By 1994, it had grown to 76,500 members in Howard and surrounding counties, including 3,000 Medicaid recipients who had been added the year before. This turned out to be the plan's peak enrollment.

A new chief operating officer at that time told the Baltimore Sun: "This organization embodies health care reform."

In 1997, data from the National Committee for Quality Assurance led U.S. News and World Report to rank CMP No. 8 among the top 10 HMOs in the U.S.

At that time, CMP had 120 full-time physicians and another 400 employees. Some of that "quality" was attributed to the managed care and tracking systems for patients in the group practice. By then the plan was occupying two large buildings at Twin Knolls North at Routes 175 and 29 next to the Thunder Hill neighborhood.

25 years with the Plan

For 25 years, I, my wife and the two daughters born in Columbia were part of one of the best health maintenance organizations in the nation, seeing great doctors, nurses, nurse practitioners and other health professionals. Early on in 1977, I got to meet one of the great orthopedic surgeons in town, Dr. Eugene "Pebble" Willis. He set my broken wrist one night after I slipped on ice as I was cleaning off my car to go to a meeting.

There were safeguards in the plan, too. When I was diagnosed with gallstones after some pain, one plan surgeon, a former Army doc, recommended removing my gallbladder. That was back in the day when that involved a major incision in the abdomen, not the laparoscopic surgery common today. I consulted the head of the surgery department. He told me that if the gallbladder wasn't giving me a lot of trouble, there was no need for surgery. I've still got my gallbladder and an occasional twinge.

My wife, Maureen Kelley, remembers the great pediatric care our daughters Sarah and Rachel received. And there was no schlepping to the Giant or Walgreens for a prescription, with a pharmacy in the same plan facility.

In 1993, I had my most intense medical experience that started with a visit to Urgent Care and high blood pressure. When my heart produced an irregular EKG, I was shipped off to Howard County General Hospital, which by that time had its own cardiac care unit. After a day or two there (memories are vague), I was carted off to Johns Hopkins in East Baltimore for a cardiac catheterization; nothing requiring further surgery in my heart was found. Still grogged up from the anesthetic, I did get to experience being a brief case study on grand rounds, with an esteemed faculty cardiologist explaining my condition to a group of young docs.

A year later, Sarai (who had changed her first name in middle school) developed a collapsed lung playing field hockey that eventually led to a two-week stay in an adolescent unit at Hopkins.

Both of these intensive hospital stays, including ambulance rides, multiple tests and surgical procedures, cost virtually nothing except for incidentals like phones. I do recall seeing an itemized accounting for Sarai from Hopkins that was more than $15,000.

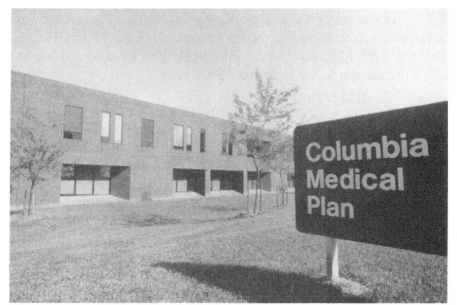

The Columbia Medical Plan in the late 1970s moved down Little Patuxent Parkway from the hospital. Photo: Courtesy Columbia Archives.

Things began to unravel at the Medical Plan in the late 1990s, and the storyline becomes confusing as the names of the principal players change. Health insurance and health care in general were then and still are in desperate search of ways to reduce costs and improve coverage.

In 1998, Blue Cross Blue Shield of Maryland and Washington became CareFirst, and that insurer merged the Columbia Medical Plan with its Freestate health maintenance organization. The Patuxent Medical Group was delivering the medical services, and by 2000, what had been the Columbia Medical Plan was down to 60,000 members and losing patients as they sought greater choice of physicians. As physicians and staff were laid off, waits got longer and more members left.

Of course, though thousands of Columbians had joined the Columbia Medical Plan over the years, many thousands of others had signed up with traditional insurance plans and saw the hundreds of doctors who practiced in Columbia and Howard County.

101

Almost all of these docs, in whatever kind of practice, would have privileges in the county's one hospital, Howard County General. That there would be just one hospital in Howard County was a matter of intense dispute for more than a decade.

The hospital

The Columbia Medical Plan fell under the umbrella of the Columbia Hospital and Clinics Foundation, run by Hopkins with Connecticut General financing. As initially conceived, the hospital was primarily to care for members of the Columbia Medical Plan, with some limited number of beds available to the wider community.

This was tough medicine to swallow for the folks outside Columbia. The county was providing the town's public schools, its public library, maintaining its public roads, its police and fire protection. Yet, a major community institution the county lacked, a hospital, was to be off limits to those who would not join the new-fangled health maintenance organization. So much for Columbia being a boon to those outside it.

This led at first to two other competing proposals for hospitals in Howard County. One came from the Sisters of Bon Secours, a French-born health care religious order whose U.S. motherhouse is still in Marriottsville. It operates Bon Secours Hospital in West Baltimore.

The other was from Lutheran Hospital, also in Baltimore, with a plan to build a hospital on Gray Rock farm owned by Charlie Miller, one of the Republican commissioners who had approved the plans to build Columbia. The farm sat next to the library on Frederick Road in Ellicott City.

The Bon Secours nuns had acquired land north of Ellicott City for a hospital, nursing home and senior housing. Back in 1973, as the Columbia hospital was about to open, the sisters had put together a proposal for the second hospital and asked the state for a certificate of need. In an environment of greater government involvement in health insurance and rate setting, state officials had to approve any new health facility.

"We thought we had it locked up," recalled Vic Broccolino, then the chief financial officer at Bon Secours Hospital, later its president and then president of Howard County General for 23 years.

Like most Catholic hospitals, the sisters refused to provide abortions. What's more, they refused to even refer women to other facilities for abortions, Broccolino said. State officials refused to issue their certificate of need.

These officials did grant approval to Lutheran, however.

As this was happening, the Columbia Hospital and Clinics Foundation had opened its 59-bed facility at Cedar Lane and Little Patuxent Parkway in July 1973. But hospital leaders were also contemplating its future. Ron Carlson, who would serve 11 years on the hospital board, recalled Hal Cohen, longtime head of Maryland's Health Services Cost Review Commission, saying, "If there is a second hospital, your financing will not allow you to survive."

Two warring camps developed, one led by Miller favoring the second hospital, and the other the Citizens Committee for Sensible Hospital Planning, a group opposing Lutheran's plan. This was one of the first steps in political involvement by Liz Bobo, later to serve as a Howard County Council member, county executive and state delegate, and Angie Beltram, later elected to the County Council herself. The battles were fought in the newspapers and mind-numbing hearings at state agencies and local boards.

The Columbia Hospital board decided to transform itself into a community hospital with a community board. After some internal debate, it dropped Columbia from its name, and in 1974, the facility became Howard County General Hospital.

The following year, the County Council, elected with the strong support of Columbia residents, passed a rezoning law that prohibited a hospital from being built on Charlie Miller's Gray Rock farm. Over the strong objections of Lutheran Hospital officials, who called it "very, very unjust," in June, the state health systems agency refused to recertify its certificate of need for a second Howard County hospital.

In 1978, the state approved a 120-bed expansion to Howard County General. The need was evident since the hospital had been leasing two floors of the Lorien Nursing Home, down Cedar Lane, for patients.

The limitations of a 59-bed hospital were painfully clear in October 1979 when Sarah Lazarick came into the world after a long and difficult labor. As she arrived, three weeks late, the Apgar score for her physical condition was 2 out of 10, then 4 out of 10. She was being worked on intensely across the delivery room, and since the small Columbia hospital had no neonatal intensive care unit, the infant with a full head of dark hair was taken by ambulance to Saint Agnes's newborn ICU.

Even though she had aspirated amniotic fluid, she looked a lot better than some of the other babies, many of them preemies. The first chance I got to hold my baby daughter, conceived and born in Columbia, was in Baltimore.

Broccolino arrives

No evidence of the small, conflicted beginnings of Howard County General Hospital remains on the massive campus it has become, surrounded by professional office buildings for medical practices. HCGH now has 264 beds, a 2016 budget of more than $235 million, and it needs a parking garage for its 1,900 full- and part-time employees. In 2016, it served more than 220,000 people, as patients, outpatients and emergency room patrons. Almost 3,600 babies were born in fiscal 2016— more than 100,000 since it opened in 1973— and any seriously ill babies can be cared for in the Lundy Family NICU since 1990.

That's the year Vic Broccolino became president, becoming the public face of the hospital for 23 years. "I was blessed that I got the job," Broccolino said in a 2016 interview. "The patients in Howard County were so different than we saw in Bon Secours," where he had been serving as president.

"The biggest challenge providing health care out here is the expectations of the people," Broccolino said. The residents know what they should be getting from their health care providers.

He said the hospital board gave him three tasks: "Improve our visibility in the community; make peace with the medical staff; and make some money."

It turns out that despite the highest occupancy rate for a Maryland hospital and a well-insured community, HCGH in its 17 years had barely turned a profit and "the debt service was huge," with the highest debt ratio for a hospital in the state. "Every project was financed," Broccolino said.

He also discovered lingering hostility from the two-hospital fight in the 1970s. People in western Howard County told him: "We will never use your hospital." That included a top business executive he eventually recruited to the board. Broccolino told the man: "If you have a heart attack, the ambulance is going to take you here."

He also found that the administrators lacked engagement with community organizations, and insisted that "everybody in the administration had to serve on two boards."

Sold to Hopkins

By 1995, the nonprofit hospital had shown a net profit of $3.5 million, and its facilities and services continued to grow. In 1996 it was clear that, with the wave of mergers and acquisitions that was sweeping the country among both nonprofit and for-profit hospitals, "we were going to get sucked up" into a bigger system at some point, Broccolino said. The board decided: "Now is the time to make our move."

The hospital hired Morgan Stanley's unit on health care mergers and acquisitions as a consultant and sent an RFP to 22 hospital corporations. It received 16 responses to the HCGH's request for proposals— "they had to do a lot of work" to respond, Broccolino said. Over the course of time, a nine-member hospital board committee narrowed it down to three choices: Johns Hopkins, Saint Agnes and Universal, a Pennsylvania for-profit.

The board committee wrangled over the options, and finally Broccolino asked the question: "Which of these institutions will be around in 50 years?"

The Johns Hopkins Health System, whose predecessor had played a key role in starting the hospital, was the obvious choice.

None of this internal process had been made public. When the announcement of the Hopkins purchase was made, many people in Columbia and Howard County were upset at being kept in the dark, including an editorial writer at the Columbia Flier. As past or future patients, they felt they had been sold without their permission.

The hospital board chairman at the time, Al Scavo, of the Rouse Co., conceded, "It's emotional, it's traumatic, and it deals with change."

In the deal, Johns Hopkins "paid" $142 million, taking on all the hospital's debt. More than half of that, $73 million, would be used to endow a community health foundation to fund and promote health initiatives exclusively in Howard County.

As Broccolino explains, it was really a leveraged buyout. Hopkins in essence took a mortgage out on the hospital's assets and promised to pay off the debt— with the revenues from Howard County General. Hopkins was on the hook, but the money would actually be repaid by the patients.

Healthy county

People in Columbia and Howard County start out with lots of advantages. That was obvious to Dr. Peter Beilenson when County Executive Ken Ulman recruited him in 2007 to be the county health officer after 13 years as health commissioner in Baltimore, a city beset with violence, teen pregnancy, lead poisoning, drug addiction and poor primary care.

His offices were just 12 miles apart, but "I went from the fifth poorest [jurisdiction] to the third wealthiest county" in the country, Beilenson said in a 2016 interview. "You had to find things to work on in public health" in Howard County.

Beilenson describes a "four-legged stool for a healthy community."

1. Safe, affordable housing;
2. Access to health care and healthy foods;

3. A decent public school system that prepares students for today's economy;

4. Access to livable wage jobs.

By all these measures, Howard County is "vastly healthier" than Baltimore and many other areas. "The ZIP code you grow up in affects the outcomes you have in your whole life," said Beilenson.

Giving access to health care to the uninsured became a major goal, leading Ulman and Beilenson to set up the Healthy Howard program. Beilenson says it reached "probably half the uninsured," households making $75,000 or less. That was eventually preempted by the Affordable Care Act, and "I was bored silly," so he turned to developing Evergreen Health, a new nonprofit model under the ACA.

Besides the strong four legs of a healthy community, Beilenson noted that Howard also has a strong network of nonprofit organizations through the Association of Community Services. Scores of groups provide a network of support beyond the traditional health care providers. In Howard County, "People were very collaborative" in solving problems, he said, much more so than in Baltimore.

Over the years, an array of alternative health organizations emphasizing holistic and nontraditional approaches to health and wellness have blossomed here, as well. One of those is the Maryland University of Integrative Health, now located in Maple Lawn, which was founded in Columbia in 1974 as the College of Chinese Acupuncture, and renamed the Tai Sophia Institute in 2000. It now offers fully accredited graduate degrees in acupuncture, oriental medicine, holistic health and herbal studies.

The Horizon Foundation

Broccolino said the $73 million paid by Johns Hopkins that endowed what became the Horizon Foundation was the "biggest payoff" Morgan Stanley had seen to that point.

Looking at what Horizon does to promote community wellness points out how backward a narrative on health can become when it emphasizes only hospitals, physicians and health insurance. That story line tends to emphasize what happens when people get sick, as opposed to stressing how they can stay well— a gap the original Columbia Medical Plan tried to bridge.

As head of the Horizon Foundation, which is the only independent health foundation in Maryland, Nikki Highsmith Vernick dissents from Beilenson on some points. "I find there's plenty of work to do in Howard County," Vernick said in an interview. "Our public health status is no different than anyone else. ... We have significant disparities in health."

Vernick is only the second director of the foundation that was headed for its first 14 years by Richard Krieg and now holds about $85 million in assets. Through 2015, it awarded more than $45 million in grants to a broad array of community organizations and initiatives. Among those were grants that helped set up the Columbia Center of Chase Brexton Health Services, Howard County's first federally qualified health center where low-income and uninsured residents can find comprehensive care— in a building once occupied by the Columbia Medical Plan.

When Vernick arrived at Horizon in 2012, the board developed a new strategic plan that focused on promoting positive lifestyles and increasing access to high quality health care. The foundation has continued grant-making to Howard County organizations and agencies, but it has decided to concentrate on several main initiatives, while weaning some organizations from its support.

One of Horizon's key goals is reducing obesity, with a particular emphasis on curtailing consumption of soda and sweetened drinks. Why obesity? When you look at the county's health statistics, Vernick said, "everything is green, and that one is red." In the last four years, Howard County's consumption of sugared beverages has declined by 20%, she said. "That's two or three times" the rate of decline in the U.S. as a whole.

Another focus is behavioral health, which is always underfunded. "We don't have as many community mental health centers as we should," Vernick said. "Most of our psychologists and psychiatrists do not take insurance."

That's why Horizon partnered with the Howard County Mental Health Authority and Way Station, a nonprofit agency, to aid residents experiencing mental health crises, regardless of income.

Horizon also wants to increase the availability of sports programs to all children. "I worry that we've created a pay-to-play system" of private youth sports leagues, said Vernick. She would like to see more after-school sports offered as well as sports programs in middle schools.

Horizon has also established an initiative to tackle one of my pet peeves about Columbia since I began covering business here: its lack of walkability (and bikeability too), an absence particularly obvious in Columbia's office and industrial parks. "You can't walk there from here" could be said about many places in Columbia, despite 94 miles of pathways, largely through woods and open space areas. Horizon calls its program Open Streets, and wants the county to invest $3 million in safe bikeways along county roads. Horizon and its biking allies were very disappointed when County Executive Allan Kittleman only put $600,000 in his fiscal 2018 capital budget for bikeways.

Overall, Vernick doesn't disagree that Columbia and the county are already a very healthy place.

"We have built a pretty amazing health care system in Howard County," she said. "We have all these amazing institutions of health."

AT MASS

Baptism is a power inside us.
The Holy Spirit is with us and in us.
He helps us every day.
At Mass we celebrate our Baptism.
We receive more of its power.

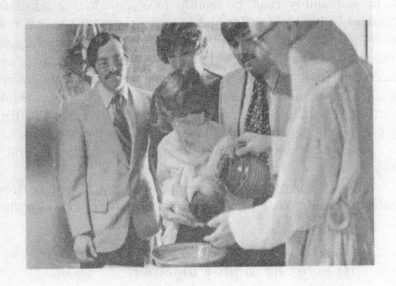

PRAYER

Dear God, thank You for my Baptism.
You are my Father.
Jesus is my big brother.
Teach me to pray as Jesus did.

74

Chapter 8:
Religion - Interfaith centers sought to bring congregations together

I could hear the chanting from the Sabbath services of Temple Isaiah down the hall of The Meeting House in Oakland Mills as our family gathered in the Catholic chapel for the baptism of Sarah Kelley Lazarick on Dec. 1, 1979.

How fitting that the Torah's God of Abraham, Isaac and Jacob was being worshipped at the same time and place as the baptism of Sarah, the name of Abraham's wife and Isaac's mother. I had called repeatedly on the God of Abraham, Isaac and Jacob after her difficult birth five weeks before as the distressed infant was whisked away in an ambulance from Howard County General Hospital to Saint Agnes Hospital's Neonatal Intensive Care Unit, as I described in chapter 7.

Now home and healthy, Sarah was being baptized by her great-uncle, Father Bennet Kelley, C.P., as she wore the same family christening gown that the priest had worn at his own baptism 57 years before. Opposite is a page Father Kelley put in a catechism he wrote for children published four years later, including a photo of Sarah Kelley Lazarick's baptism. From right are Father Kelley, Len Lazarick, Maureen Kelley holding Sarah, godparents Kathy Lazarick and Kevin Kelley, my sister and Maureen's brother.

I really liked the idea that Sarah was being brought into the church in a welcoming community where Christians of different denominations and Jews as well shared space and ideas.

This was unheard of when I was growing up. My mother was Presbyterian, and she and my Catholic father were married in the rectory and not the church because it was a "mixed" marriage.

It was not until the mid-1960s that a shared facility like this was even conceivable for Catholics, when the Second Vatican Council adopted the Declaration on Religious Liberty. That was largely due to the long-suppressed work of Jesuit theologian John Courtney Murray, who taught at the Woodstock theological seminary just 14 miles away across the Patapsco River, where he is also buried. The declaration opened the way to broad ecumenical cooperation and interfaith dialogue.

These interfaith centers in Wilde Lake and Oakland Mills, the first religious facilities built in the planned new town, were among the unique features most often remarked on with wonder in media coverage of Columbia.

While they were consistent with the open, integrated and forward-thinking city Jim Rouse had in mind, they were only a vague idea in the original planning process. There was no expert on religion in the original planning group that included expertise in so many other fields—education, health, government, sociology, economics. Rouse may have been his own expert on religion.

Rouse's religious motivation

As Josh Olsen documents in his essential biography of Rouse, "Better Places, Better Lives," religion was at the core of Rouse's motivation to build a new city, starting with a 1961 talk he gave on "Christianity and the American City." Like my mother, Rouse and his wife Libby were practicing Presbyterians, and Jim Rouse was even an elder at his Baltimore church. In the 1960s, as Columbia was being conceived and planned, the Rouses were also regular participants in the Church of the Savior in Washington, D.C., a nontraditional congregation that strongly embraced the social gospel of Jesus.

In 1964, as the acquisition of land was being announced, Rouse and his staff invited the local churches in to help drum up local support for the project's zoning, but they approached the national denominations as well.

This set off a long, complicated and sensitive process of talks and negotiations. Letters and memos went back and forth, filling three thick volumes of documents at the Columbia Archives.

The Protestant groups took the lead, some more enthusiastic than others. This culminated two years later with the creation of the Columbia Religious Facilities Corporation on May 31, 1966.

"It was the Protestants who first developed the interfaith center concept," said Carolyn Arena, a member of St. John the Evangelist Catholic parish who served on the board of the Religious Facilities

Corporation for years. Arena is putting the final touches on a book she co-edited with the late Betty Martin on the interfaith experience in Columbia, with contributions from 40 different people of various congregations.

Howard Research and Development, the Rouse subsidiary building Columbia, was willing to sell the land for churches at bargain prices.

"The village centers were going to be the center of life in Columbia," Arena said, and that's where the churches wanted to be. In the First Village, as it was called before it was dubbed Wilde Lake, HRD wanted to put the churches on a high point west of the village center. The churches wanted 10 acres to the east, which they finally got.

Catholics finally join

While there had been Catholic representatives at some of the meetings, the Catholic Church was going through immense changes in liturgy and outlook after Vatican II, and the Church wasn't committed to participate in the joint facilities. Then, in 1967, Wallace Hamilton, Rouse's director of institutional planning, wrote, "Hell has frozen over—the Catholics agree to join." Josh Olsen in his biography says there was an earlier meeting between Rouse and Cardinal Lawrence Shehan in which the Baltimore archbishop approved of the idea.

The Unitarians with some trepidation came on board, and the first Jewish congregations in Howard County also agreed to join. (The few Jews who lived in Howard County had been mostly merchants in Ellicott City.)

Cardinal Shehan also agreed to foot a third of the costs of the facility that was to be built in a few years.

According to Hamilton, in the planning process for the churches, "The one conviction the committee held through thick and thin was that they were not going to build a cathedral or any other ceremonial bricks and mortar."

A brochure for Columbia's first residents explained that religious services would be held for several years at Slayton House, the Wilde Lake community center that would be the launching pad for other faith communities in future years.

"This may seem, at first glance, to be a haphazard and stopgap arrangement," but it was the outcome of three years of planning, the brochure said. This was part of "an adventure in new forms of congregational involvement with the life of a community, new forms of ministry, new forms of interdenominational and interfaith cooperation—all in the hope that it will lead the people and the congregations of Columbia to explore new imperatives of God's relationship to man and men's relationship to each other."

There was a practical and financial reason for the decision. "Sometimes up to 4/5 of total income [of a congregation] are spent on the building and maintaining of a physical plant of a church or synagogue."

The opening of the Wilde Lake Interfaith Center in September 1971. Photo Courtesy Columbia Archives.

Not a cathedral

Certainly, no cathedral was envisioned. The architecture of the first building, the Wilde Lake Interfaith Center that opened in 1971, reflected the architectural equivalent of the lowest common denominator for this motley crew of priests, ministers and rabbis in a hodgepodge of congregations worshipping under the same roof. It still looks more like a utilitarian office building than a church. Inside, when it first opened, it had the same nondenominational feel, and to an extent it still does.

For Catholics, and perhaps others, the worship space was the most unsettling in what was to be their permanent home. Room 1, the largest space in Wilde Lake, was as generic as its name. No statues, no pews, no kneelers, no stained glass, no marble, and perhaps most jarring for those who had only recently switched to worshipping in English rather than Latin, there was no tabernacle, the typically ornate repository for the Holy Eucharist. There were just chairs, an altar table and a cross.

No need to genuflect, folks; Jesus in the form of bread wafers was stored in a tabernacle across the hall in a small chapel.

Room 1 and Room 4 were deliberately utilitarian so they could be used by other faith traditions and for community meetings and events, as they often are.

Into this space in June 1977, 10 years after Columbia and St. John the Evangelist parish opened for business, walked its new pastor, a 37-year-old priest named Richard Tillman.

When he got the call from the archdiocese at the South Baltimore parishes he was serving, "I was really shocked" at the unexpected assignment, Tillman recalled in a 2017 interview. He had participated in the Central Maryland Ecumenical Council, but he had only served in traditional parishes. He was also a bit surprised that the priestly personnel director asked him how his celibacy was going—the vow not to marry.

"They were looking for some stability," said Tillman. The first pastor, John Walsh, had left the priesthood to marry, and the current pastor, George Cora, was about to do the same.

If the church was looking for stability—it turned out Archbishop William Borders had suggested him for the job—they got it in spades with Tillman. He would serve 33 years as pastor, four times as long as most Catholic pastors, doubling the parish in size to 3,000 families.

"They knew I liked it here," Tillman said. "Once I got here and found out what was going on, I liked it here."

Catholic priests had dealt with interdenominational ministry as chaplains in the military and at public universities, but Columbia was a special case.

The 1970s and '80s were perhaps the high points of interfaith cooperation and what was then known as the Columbia Cooperative Ministry, which was involved in social ministry as well, such as the Interfaith Housing Corp. it set up.

The Catholics were operating out of both Wilde Lake and The Meeting House in Oakland Mills, which opened in 1975. In Wilde Lake, there was St. John Baptist Church, an African-American congregation of Baptists; St. John United Methodist/Presbyterian Church, already interdenominational and home church for Jim Rouse and his second wife Patty; and a Lutheran congregation. Oakland Mills had other Christian and Jewish congregations, as it still does today.

It was in The Meeting House that I experienced my first Bat Mitzvah, the Jewish coming of age ritual for the daughter of a friend; decades later, in the same room, my daughter Sarai would be married at a Catholic mass celebrated by Father Tillman. That day, when I showed Tillman a picture of him and Sarai taken after her first communion in Wilde Lake, he went into the sacristy and found the same multicolored stole he was wearing that day 20 years before.

Sharing with other faiths

Tillman remembered how, in his early years in Wilde Lake, "four or five of us pastors would get together to discuss our sermons," based on the same readings from the standard lectionary. "Faith has that interfaith dimension built into it," Tillman said, and in his own homilies, he would bring in perspectives from other traditions with "different approaches to faith."

The interfaith centers were a good solution to the problem of startup congregations in a new community. But as the congregations prospered, they began crowding each other and outgrowing the space.

Rev. Dr. Robert Turner arrived from Cambridge, Mass., on May 1, 1993, to pastor St. John Baptist Church, in hopes of working with others. "I was intrigued by this concept of the planned community, and even more intrigued by the interfaith centers," Turner said in a 2017 interview.

Once he arrived, he found that there was little shared ministry beyond an occasional exchange of pulpits. And as the ministries for his own congregation grew, there was increased competition for space in Wilde Lake, not just on Sundays but in the evenings as well.

"The space was impeding our growth," and in 1997, his congregation left Wilde Lake for a sojourn in a Route 108 office park.

His was not the last religious community to find a home in Columbia's first business park.

10 villages, 4 true interfaith centers

In the 10 villages that make up Columbia, there are only four true interfaith centers where two or more congregations share the same facilities.

The near-vacant Long Reach Village Center comes alive on Sunday mornings for three energetic, praiseful services in music and word at the Celebration Church, a successor to the Long Reach Church of God founded by Bishop Robert Davis and now with his son Robbie Davis as the lead pastor.

There were two congregations originally slated for the Long Reach site, but after the other dropped out, the church opened in 1973. It now has 2,500 predominantly African-American members and a day school.

In 2005, after a long struggle, the Gathering Place, the River Hill interfaith center, opened with two congregations—the Emmanuel Messianic Jewish Congregation, which observes Jewish traditions but accepts Jesus as the messiah; and the Oak Ridge Community Church, which worshipped in Howard County schools for years. Emmanuel first bought the land from the Rouse Co. in 1998.

At Kings Contrivance Village Center, instead of one facility, there are two churches on one site. The Orthodox Church of St. Matthew, like other startups, made a stop in Slayton House, then built its own church, in modern style but resplendent with icons and murals, where it began worshipping in 2007. Its Divine Liturgy on Sundays is chanted in English but with typical Eastern tonalities, elaborate vestments and abundant incense. Next door in a separate building is Cornerstone Church, a predominantly African-American congregation. They share a parking lot.

The Owen Brown Interfaith Center is now the most eclectic of the centers. Opened in 1984—nine years after The Meeting House—it became the permanent home for a United Methodist congregation and the Unitarian-Universalists, a group that honors all religions. Both had been renting space in Columbia. It now also includes small congregations of Muslims, Jews and followers of Sathya Sai Baba, an Indian who embraces many religions. A 2016 addition provides one of the nicer sanctuaries.

In 1986, the Columbia Flier did a survey that found that only 44 percent of Columbians who chose to worship at all worshipped in an interfaith center.

Outside the interfaith centers

Many of the others went to the churches that existed before Columbia. Perhaps the oldest is Christ Episcopal Church on Oakland Mills Road at Dobbin, sometimes called Old Brick for the 1809 structure that is the oldest church building in Howard County. There has been a church on this site since 1711, but like many a church serving Columbia, the congregation that worships at the newer, larger sanctuary on the grounds bills itself as "diverse, multicultural."

Catholics looking for a more traditional experience have long flocked to one of the oldest parishes in Howard County, St. Louis, in Clarksville. It grew out of the private chapel at Doughoreagan Manor, just north of Columbia, the country home of Charles Carroll, the only Catholic signer of the Declaration of Independence. The Carroll chapel was built in the 1700s when it was illegal to build a Catholic church in the colony.

Responding to Howard County's growth, including the nearby village of River Hill, Columbia's last, St. Louis is now on its fourth church building, each one larger than the last. The 2006 church that serves 4,200 families is more cathedral-like than any worship space in Howard County. The stained-glass windows were brought from the Basilica of the Assumption in Baltimore, the first cathedral in the United States, after its original plain windows were restored.

A choir singing in several languages leads the service at Bridgeway Community Church on Jan. 15, 2017. Photo: Len Lazarick.

Within Columbia itself, there are likely more worshipers in business parks, schools and community centers than there are in the interfaith buildings.

Bridgeway

The largest and most remarkable, with a reach far beyond Columbia, is Bridgeway Community Church, operating out of a large complex on Red Branch Road in the former headquarters of Head Sports.

On any Sunday morning, the cars stream in off of Route 108, filling three parking lots; congregants occupy most of the seats for three services in a theater-like auditorium that seats 1,047 people. On a Sunday early in 2017, the hall rocked with song in five languages, with a choir as ethnically diverse as the people who packed the hall.

"Our goal was to be a multicultural army in Columbia," said Rich Becker, a co-founder of the church nearly 25 years ago with Senior Pastor David Anderson. "We wanted to work hard to create a church that people wanted to come to...a place that wouldn't be boring."

The church specifically embraces a "multicultural ministry," the title of a book Anderson penned. It followed a book he wrote called "Gracism," which executive pastor Dave Michener explained is "the opposite of racism." Anderson is African-American, Becker and Michener are white, reflecting the deliberate ethnic mix of their ministry, now staffed by 40 people in many shades from pale pink to dark brown.

"There were a lot of naysayers [to us] as a multicultural church," Michener said. The congregation now includes people from 52 countries and about half are black—American, African and Caribbean.

"I get to see God in many different groups," Anderson told the congregation on the weekend of Martin Luther King's Birthday.

Bridgeway had modest beginnings. Like many of Columbia's first congregations, it started with services in Slayton House, where it stayed for five years. There were 110 people on hand that Easter Sunday in 1992. "The following week we had 30 people," Becker recalled. It was slow going.

Both Anderson and Becker had to work outside jobs to support themselves while they built the church.

The diversity they were seeking to build in their church is "one of the main reasons that we chose to be in Columbia," Becker said. When people come to worship, they want to make sure "they see someone who represents them."

The church is nondenominational, but its beliefs are standard Bible-based evangelical Christianity. "We actually talk about real life," in our sermons, said Michener. "We want people to have an experience of community," and "we want to remove any unnecessary barriers" for people coming to church.

Michener said that in addition to the thousand present in the auditorium, as many as 2,000 watch online, from different countries as well. (With the advances in Internet technology and reduced equipment costs, many other congregations live stream their services, including the Catholics in Wilde Lake.)

Anderson also has a daily radio show broadcast, "Real Talk with Dr. David Anderson," from a fully equipped digital studio in the church complex, and he does TV shows as well from the studio.

Michener said they are getting ready to launch other campuses for the church. But "the bigger we get, the smaller we want to feel," he said.

Besides traditional churches and synagogues that have grown around Columbia, there are more places of worship in business settings, such as Bethany Church on Dobbin Road in a former warehouse space once occupied by Cornerstone Community Church. "We're here to build the kingdom of God," said its young pastor, C.J. Matthews, who has ambitious plans to build up the church from its 105 members.

Not far from Bridgeway, in flex office space off of Rumsey Road, is the Maryum Islamic Center, founded by Imam Mahmoud Abdel-Hady, who led the larger Dar Al-Taqwa mosque on Route 108 for 19 years. He preaches to about 100 men and women at Friday prayer. It never would have occurred to the early Columbia planners that Muslims would need a place to worship here.

'Missed opportunity'

Before Pastor Turner and his growing Baptist congregation left the Wilde Lake Interfaith Center 20 years ago, "we looked for some space in Columbia, but we couldn't afford five acres in Columbia." The Rouse Co. was unbending. Turner had even approached Jim Rouse, long gone from the firm that bore his name, for his help. But Rouse told him, "He intended for these interfaith communities to solve the problem for themselves."

That's when Turner moved the church to the Route 108 business park. It eventually bought 40 acres in Ellicott City on Marriottsville Road across from Turf Valley at a price "for less than five acres in Columbia," Turner said. But the county would not extend water and sewer to the property.

In time, the Howard County school system approached Turner as it hunted for a school site in Ellicott City. It was willing to swap 10 acres in Columbia for his 40 acres and some cash.

The noon "contemporary" service at St. John the Baptist Church on Jan. 22, 2017. Photo: Len Lazarick

At the corner of Tamar Drive and Route 175, St. John Baptist built the most visible church on new town land, a structure that actually looks like a church, outside and in, steeple and all, with pews and pulpit. It opened in 2009.

Yet his leaving the Wilde Lake Interfaith Center 20 years ago "was bittersweet. I really wanted to do some creative things with different denominations."

Turner has been a leader in the formation of PATH, People Acting Together in Howard, a group of congregations mostly in Columbia that includes Catholics, Protestants, Jews and even the Muslims at the Maryum Center. They hosted a meeting at the Wilde Lake Interfaith Center in January 2017 to push for making Howard a sanctuary county—as both Turner and Abdel-Hady urged their congregations to do.

Yet, "there's still no shared ministry," Turner said. "I think that is a missed opportunity."

"They are so wrapped up in fulfilling their individual faith community mission that they don't spend time in exploring a shared faith vision. There isn't a sense of 'we.'"

And while the congregations focus on their own communities, there is also a consciousness of the larger populace in Columbia that is un-churched. "Our biggest competition in Columbia is athletics" on Saturday and Sunday, Turner said.

Catholics have largely taken over the Wilde Lake center with an influx of Hispanics and Latinos over the past decade. In addition to the center's three masses in English each weekend, three masses are celebrated there in Spanish, with the service for the small St. John United Methodist/Presbyterian congregation sandwiched in between. (After the 2008 recession hit, the Methodist/Presbyterian group abandoned plans to build a freestanding church—cross and all—next to the current facility.)

Remnants of interfaith sharing remain. At a Sunday mass in October 2016, I noticed that the Stations of the Cross had been taken down in the room—14 modernistic wood carvings evoking Jesus's Way of the Cross that were a recent addition to the bland brick walls. At choir practice the next day, I noticed the large crucifix over the altar and the one statue of the Holy Family had been removed. Then it hit me—it was Rosh Hashanah. The Catholics again were accommodating the Jewish congregations that swell for the High Holy Days.

While the realities of religious division remain, there is still in Columbia and in many other places across the land—that spirit of interracial and interfaith diversity that bloomed in the Civil Rights movement and Columbia's early days.

We heard again at Bridgeway on that MLK Birthday Sunday the conclusion of Martin Luther King's 1963 speech at the Lincoln Memorial, in his own voice a speech, like other King speeches, that Jim Rouse had circulated among colleagues and friends in the 1960s.

"From every state and every city, we will be able to speed up that day when all of God's children, black men and white men, Jews and gentiles, Protestants and Catholics, will be able to join hands and sing in the words of the old Negro spiritual, 'Free at last! Free at last! Thank God Almighty, we are free at last!'"

The man-made Wilde Lake and its village looking southeast toward the mall on May 2, 2017. Photo: Brent Myers Aerial Photography for Len Lazarick.

Opposite: This aerial view taken in the 1960s shows the land that would become Columbia's Town Center looking south down two-lane Route 29 running diagonally on left. This includes the land shown in the photo above from a different angle. In the foreground is what was then Allview Golf Course, now redeveloped as Fairhills Golf Club. What would become the Village of Wilde Lake is on the right and the Village of Oakland Mills on the left. Visible at the horizon are the older subdivisions of Sebring on the right of 29 and Allview Estates on the left. Photo: Courtesy Columbia Archives.

Chapter 9:
Environment - Respecting the land while building a city

"To respect the land" was one of the four basic goals for Columbia often repeated by developer Jim Rouse more than 50 years ago as he pitched his proposal "to build a complete city" on 14,000 acres of farmland, woods and stream valleys.

The goals seem almost a contradiction. If he wanted to "respect the land," why not just leave the fields and forest as they were?

Howard County's population had barely grown at all since the Civil War, but it had doubled to 51,000 in 15 years by the time Columbia got underway.

If the county's fields and woods were to be developed, as everyone expected, there was a better way to do it, Rouse insisted, one that would integrate nature into a network of neighborhoods and villages connected by pathways, many along the streams that would be forever protected.

This may seem obvious in the 21st century, but in the early 1960s, Rouse and his planners were on the cutting edge of landscape design. The planners used overlays to show stands of trees, streambeds and steep land where development would be difficult.

"It was a completely different way of thinking, especially on the scale of planning for a community of 100,000 people," said Chick

Rhodehamel, long-time vice president for open space management for the Columbia Association, in a 2009 interview with Barbara Kellner of the Columbia Archives. "That was monumental."

Columbia was being laid out at the dawning of the environmental movement. Rouse said later that, when the first plans for Columbia were approved, "there was little concern about environmental issues as we now understand them."

The Environmental Protection Agency didn't exist; there was no national environmental policy, no Earth Day, and the Chesapeake Bay Foundation had just been formed in 1967 when Columbia's first residents moved in. It took years for its slogan "Save the Bay" to become widely accepted in Maryland.

Surveying in suburbia

Even as a teenager in the 1960s, I had direct experience of how traditional suburban housing developments happened. "And they're all made out of ticky-tacky, and they all look just the same," sang Pete Seeger in his 1963 ditty "Little Boxes."

I grew up in Bucks County, Pa., a few miles south of the second Levittown, a huge, 1950s suburb. For four summers, from 1963 to 1966, I worked as a chain-and-rod man on a surveying crew for my godfather's civil engineering firm.

One summer we would go out to woods or wheat fields, chopping line to clear sight-lines, and then map the topography. The next summer, we would be back to the same spot, staking out the roads and lots, marking the levels for the graders to flatten the land and perhaps take down some or all of the trees. Later we would return to put in stakes for the corners of the homes or apartments, and follow up the next year with a survey to establish where the buildings actually stood.

Much of that early surveying process still needed to occur in Columbia—a suburb or a city can't be built without bulldozers and graders. But the main roads and side streets were designed to follow the contours of the land where possible. There would be no grid patterns of streets, but a few main drags through each village and hundreds of cul-de-sacs. The looping roads and limited connections from one village to the next that resulted is often a source of confusion and frustration for visitors—and residents as well.

The need to name all these streets without duplication in the region, as the post office insisted, and Rouse's desire that they be named with imagination led to the many unusual street names in Columbia, subject of a 2008 book, "Oh, you must live in Columbia! The origins of place names in Columbia, Maryland."

It was not as if the land for Columbia was untouched wilderness. Most of Howard County had been covered with trees that were cleared after the first settlers arrived 300 years ago, and some of it had been farmed for centuries.

What was left of nature was not only to be preserved, but enhanced and made accessible, eventually with 94 miles of pathways—part of a community for "the growth of people." The Rouse Co. required builders to protect the trees that were left on the lots, and there were rules to prevent erosion and sediment from flowing into the streams and the rivers. Erosion of the topsoil was a centuries-old problem in Maryland, initially from farming. The town of Elkridge in the county's northeast corner had once been a deep port for sailing ships until the Patapsco River silted up in the late 18th century.

The preservation of trees was especially apparent in neighborhoods such as Swansfield, Steven's Forest, Thunder Hill and parts of Phelps Luck. And where there weren't trees on what had been open fields and pastures, builders, the developer and the Columbia Association would plant them. The figures vary as to how many trees have been planted—in 1972 alone, a Rouse Co. report said it had planted 2,434 trees, another 287 flowering trees and 3,653 evergreens—but it was certainly in the tens of thousands. There are many more trees in Columbia now than when Rouse first purchased the land, as any aerial photo shows.

The lakes

And of course, there are lakes. They may seem like an essential element of Columbia's natural landscape, but they are as artificial as a backyard pool.

On the Piedmont Plateau where all of Howard County sits, all lakes and ponds are man-made features. Columbia's three lakes are dammed up streams—the dedication of the dam at Wilde Lake on June 21, 1967, is the date we observe as Columbia's birthday. There's nothing wild about the body of water that gave its name to what the planners initially called First Village; it is named for Frazer Wilde, the chairman of Connecticut General Life Insurance Co., which financed the new town.

Wilde Lake is the smallest lake with the hardest edges. The Cove, Columbia's first apartments, and the distinctive white stucco of the Tidesfall townhouses, stand right at the edge of the lake, as do a series of custom homes where Jim Rouse lived and former CA President Pat Kennedy still does. Lake Kittamaqundi, with its Indian name, preceded all the office buildings in Town Center, and a few years later, Lake Elkhorn filled.

As Rhodehamel, first hired as CA's ecologist, described it, man-made lakes are like swimming pools and "take a lot of management. ... You're fighting the forces of nature."

Columbia lakes have several roles. Aesthetics and recreation are the most obvious. But they also have a more practical role in stormwater management and flood control. The lakes collect sediment and the nutrients that wash off all the green lawns, leading to algae blooms that suck up oxygen, killing fish and aquatic life.

As the lakes fill up, they require periodic dredging and a place to put the fertilizer-soaked soil, an annoyance to the residents who value them for natural beauty and relaxation.

Wildlife

As attractive as they are to humans, the lakes and streams also attract wildlife. Ultimately there is "more diversity than there was 50 years ago," said environmental author Ned Tillman, who lives overlooking Lake Elkhorn. There are more species of birds and mammals than were to be found in the 1960s, like the blue herons that nab fish in the shallow lakes or the red-crested pileated woodpeckers knocking on the trees.

I often find more wildlife in my yard—a couple hundred feet from miles of wooded streambed—than I do in most parks, especially now that our dog is gone and the fence is down. The critters have little to fear and even get fed by some folks, against the strong urgings of wildlife managers.

On Christmas Day 2016, there were eight deer in my backyard; my neighbor said he saw a dozen, far more than either of us has seen together before. The lack of two-legged and four-legged predators has led to an explosion in the deer population. I recall a conversation in the 1990s with ex-Sen. Jim Clark on his farm at Route 108 and Centennial Lane as we talked about the deer nuisance. Clark said he remembered his grandparents' attic full of trunks covered with deer hides—which farmers thought was a good use for a deer.

The squirrels proliferate too. Former County Administrator Ned Eakle once told me that spying a squirrel in his youth as he hunted in Elkridge was rare.

I've seen two red foxes recently scurrying down the sidewalk in my front yard—and because of them, there are not so many bunnies nibbling the grass. We haven't had mice in quite a while either, which could be gratis of the foxes or the hawk that swoops around the nearby stream. We haven't seen much of the coyote that once crossed Cradlerock Way at night.

We hosted a mama skunk and her brood of cute babies a while back under the front steps; a wildlife expert trapped them and released them far away. The dead skunk that stunk up the neighborhood after being squished by a car was not so lucky.

The vultures and blackbirds will sometimes roost on the rooftop. It's hard to say which of the many berry-eating birds 30 years ago had feasted on the wild cherry tree and then perched on a nearby fence post, doing its duty, which led to the sprouting of another wild cherry tree. It's grown into the largest tree on our quarter-acre now that the emerald ash borer has killed the towering white ash planted by Ryland more than 44 years ago. Other white ashes have survived in our neighbors' yards.

Fortunately, we are still flyover country for the Canadian geese that park themselves on the playing fields between the East Columbia library and the Lake Elkhorn Middle School, leaving their toxic poop for young soccer and baseball players.

Alas, the swans are gone from Elkhorn and Kittamaqundi, but they were mostly Eurasians never native to the area, Rhodehamel said.

The swans may have departed Lake Elkhorn, but the beavers are still chomping away, gnawing down small trees and big bushes. One wonders if they're related to the beavers that years ago blocked up our stream, creating their own little lake till someone at CA knocked it down.

In February 2017, I found a similar beaver dam on a stream that flows into the Middle Patuxent River. If Rouse had stuck to his original plan for Columbia, the site of that beaver dam would have been several feet underwater in the town's fourth and largest lake that never happened.

The Middle Patuxent

The original plan for Columbia showed Little Patuxent Parkway going straight west from the hospital. It would cross over a bridge on the Middle Patuxent River that would be dammed, creating a mile-long lake deep enough for serious water recreation, such as skiing. The road would have extended all the way through to Route 108, integrating the Village of River Hill, Columbia's last, with the original villages and downtown Columbia.

That Columbians don't have heavy-duty boating and water skiing can be blamed on Al Geis, a wildlife expert who lived on 20 acres near the river valley and studied bird behavior, including the mating habits of the woodcock. Geis persuaded Jim Rouse to come see the curious mating dance of the birds. It got Rouse to thinking about the whole Middle Patuxent area and the fowl and fauna that populated it. As he explained to the Howard County Zoning Board in 1976:

The Middle Patuxent River would have been dammed to form a mile-long lake in the original plans for Columbia. It is now the center of Howard County's largest park. Photo: Len Lazarick.

"We called upon the Department of Interior to examine the plan, and it recommended strongly against the lake because of the destruction of plant and animal life that would result and urged instead the preservation of the stream valley."

Antioch College, which had a branch in Columbia, did a further study, the Middle Patuxent Valley Association was formed, and in 1973, County Executive Ed Cochran asked "if there were some way the enlarged open space might be provided," Rouse said.

The revised plan that Rouse himself was personally pitching would create 1,021 acres—1.6 square miles—of permanent open space, 20% larger than Central Park in New York City. Columbia's total acreage is slightly smaller in land area than Manhattan, but 25% is open space, and the population is only 6% of Manhattan's.

County purchases parkland

In exchange for the developable land the company was giving up, Rouse asked the county for more density and clustering of homes on other parts of the company-owned land. The county agreed, the deal was made, and 20 years later, in 1996, the county purchased the acreage with $2.2 million from the state Open Space Program—the visionary program that passed in 1969, co-sponsored by none other than Sen. Jim Clark and his friend and fellow farmer, Senate President Bill James.

The Rouse Co. (actually it's Howard Research and Development Corp. division that was building Columbia but we usually refer to it simply as Rouse) put $1.76 million aside in a trust fund for the Middle Patuxent Environmental Foundation that co-manages the property with the county's Recreation and Parks Department.

The Middle Patuxent Environmental Area is the county's largest park, and judging by the foot traffic, probably one of the least-known and -traveled amenities in the county. This parkland comprises largely mature, second-growth upland forest and flood plain forest. Like some of the land acquired for Columbia, its northern half had been logged and farmed as far back as the 18th century by the Charles Carroll family. Some of its "meadows" are simply abandoned farm fields, replanted with native grasses.

The Middle Patuxent is touched by housing easily visible when the leaves are gone, but is home to a wide range of wildlife. That includes "about 150 species of birds, over 40 species of mammals, and numerous amphibians, reptiles, fishes, butterflies, plants and other wildlife," says its website.

We'll have to take their word for it. In mid-winter when I visited, like in any northern U.S. park, there wasn't much wildlife to be seen. There were the hanging ceramic gourds for the purple martins, bluebird boxes and netting for deer that is part of a study on Lyme disease. The most common species found on its 5-1/2 miles of unpaved hiking trails is *homo sapiens* and their canines, leashed and unleashed.

Backyard stormwater

Much as Rouse tried "to respect the land," the water that flowed through it, and the trees and bushes that grew on it, there were limitations to that respect and what builders were willing to do. According to Howard County Planning Director Tom Harris in a 1974 paper, stormwater management was "designed to speed water as rapidly as possible into the streams," not to keep much of it out of the streams as we would today.

Again, look no further than my backyard. My house is built near the top of a small slope, and six other lots send the rain that doesn't soak into the ground through slight gullies and then through my yard into a drain at the far back corner.

When that rain comes in torrents, the flow is like a river that can't be stopped. With the push to reduce polluted stormwater runoff that contains soil, fertilizer, oil and other unwanted chemicals, the county and CA have new programs to manage the runoff. For my yard, only a massive rain garden with rocks would do, unless my "upstream" neighbors put in their own rain gardens to prevent a problem they never see.

Cars and transit

An influx of 100,000 people, even with the most enlightened environmental management, creates massive amounts of impervious surfaces where people live, work, shop, play and park their cars. The automobile made Columbia possible, but it is one of its principal environmental villains.

Cars and trucks need impervious asphalt and concrete to drive and park on, and the county probably required wider streets than were necessary. Oil on the roads eventually flows into the storm sewers and into the streams; carbon and heat spew into the air, expanding the heat island that Columbia has become.

The noise from traffic intrudes on the most bucolic of scenes, like the path along the meandering Little Patuxent River and its wide flood plain southwest of Lake Elkhorn. The roar of Route 32 can be heard at great distance, though not as loud as the roar of I-95 high above on concrete stilts further downstream. About the only birds to be heard in mid-winter from the Middle Patuxent Valley are soaring jets making their ascent from BWI.

The early planners had every hope of getting people out of their cars and off the streets, not just walking and biking the paths (running for exercise was barely in its infancy), but to use transit services. Many staff-years went into designing dedicated bus routes, and even contemplating small people movers. State and federal transportation officials were lobbied and cajoled.

In 1964, there was talk of "tiny buses every five or ten minutes," no more than a three-minute walk from every residence. There was even an outlandish estimate of a daily ridership of 29,000.

The reality was much more modest when Columbia residents arrived. In 1969, Robert Bartolo, the Rouse Co.'s transportation planner, reported that "nearly every resident in Columbia had experienced or heard a 'horror story' concerning Columbia transit."

There were tales of stranded passengers, lost drivers and missing buses. Call-a-ride was more successful, but mass transit in Columbia has hobbled along from the start, much as it does today. Ridership declines, fare box revenues go down, and schedules are reduced in a vicious cycle. Only people who can't afford a car are desperate enough to take one of the half-empty buses and get to their destination a few miles away two hours later.

The Columbia Association operated the bus system for 29 years, struggling with limited resources. In 1996, it finally persuaded Howard County government to take over the bus routes.

"It takes density to do transit," said Marsha McLaughlin, former director of planning and zoning for 13 years. "But Howard County is very lucky from a road and transportation point of view. ... We have a phenomenal state road network."

Roads and highways
As much as Rouse officials worked on transit solutions for the new town, they paid even more attention to improving highway access. Old-timers like myself can recall the original traffic lights on Route 29 to get across town from Oakland Mills Road, Owen Brown Road and Route 108.

Rouse executives worked for years with state highway officials to expand lanes, build interchanges, improve signage and move traffic in and out of Columbia. Highway planning and construction often takes decades.

Jim Rouse, a major player in civic and business organizations, would contact high state officials directly. In one interesting exchange in December 1966, Gov.-Elect Spiro T. Agnew thanked Rouse for his recommendation of a person to head what was then called the State Roads Commission. Agnew signed his letter "Ted," and shortly afterward, he appointed Jerome Wolff, a Towson transportation consultant who worked for Rouse and others Agnew knew as Baltimore County executive, as head of the Roads Commission.

HRD officials strongly lobbied for expansion of Routes 29, 32 and 175 the way they wanted them, and even funded interchanges in advance to improve traffic flow. Sometimes they prevailed; other times they didn't. While the two-lane Route 29 is now a six-lane walled expressway, the traffic it carries is often just passing through Columbia, adding to the air, noise, water and heat pollution. On the other hand, without Columbia's planned shopping centers, Route 29 was destined to become crowded with the same kind of piecemeal strip development that lines Route 40 in Ellicott City.

What was much less successful were attempts to improve mass transit into and out of Columbia. An extension of the Baltimore light rail line that appears on some plans never materialized. Regional transit agencies have provided workforce transit to places such as BWI and Arundel Mills; and commuter buses into D.C. and Baltimore are often crowded, but operate only on weekdays and limited schedules. Residents are mostly dependent on cars to get to them. There is a study of bus rapid transit down Route 29 to Silver Spring, but the four-lane bridge over the Patuxent River reservoir could be a major bottleneck.

The increased density of Columbia's downtown development is supposed to provide more transit options, if only in Town Center.

While people pay attention to the streams and rivers that flow above ground, only public works officials and civil engineers pay much attention to the underground supply of water that people use to drink, bathe and flush. It comes from reservoirs far away in Baltimore

County; the wastewater departs underground largely along streambeds downhill to the sewage treatment plant in Savage. Some of that treated wastewater is now used to cool huge computers at the National Security Agency, where many Columbians work.

Judging the environment

Environmental expert Ned Tillman has been watching Columbia for decades, first from a small farm on Manor Lane just outside the town, and now perched in a condo with a grand view of Lake Elkhorn though the trees.

"Open space is probably one of the major successes of Columbia," Tillman said in an interview. "Many cities and towns did not do a good job of that."

"We have to learn to co-evolve with nature and make sure that the green infrastructure here is healthy," he said. "Howard County needs biodiversity."

Tillman has written about the big picture in his books "The Chesapeake Watershed" and "Saving the Places We Love." He advocates government action and corporate leadership, as the Rouse Co. showed, but he urges individual efforts as well.

Under the Trump administration, "one could expect the air quality is going to get worse. It's all about the overuse and use of fossil fuels," Tillman said. Much of the local air pollution comes from the heavy traffic on I-95 and coal-powered electricity plants to the west, where a lot of our local power originates.

"I've been supportive of downtown redevelopment because it is going to help fix some of the stormwater runoff problems in downtown," Tillman said. "I was glad to see Howard Hughes [Corp.] work on the Little Patuxent River streambed, which was revitalized, and how stormwater bio-filtration systems were added to the Whole Foods parking lot."

On the stormwater issues that plague many neighborhoods like my own, "The developers could have done a better job," he said, but homeowners can take action on their own. "Everybody has yet to re-landscape their backyards," though people are planting more native species.

Lake Elkhorn looking east from the dam near Broken Land Parkway. Photo: Len Lazarick

The state planning department estimates Howard County's population will grow by 50,000 people over the next 20 years, and perhaps 10,000 of them will be residents of new downtown apartments. "Our green infrastructure is going to be under stress," said Tillman.

But he noted that, while the population of the mid-Atlantic states has doubled since 1960, Howard County's has grown seven-fold. "It's incredible that we have any nature left."

But, as many Columbians could attest, nature is just outside the door or a short walk away, as Rouse planned it 50 years ago.

At the opening of the pavilion July 14, 1867, Marjorie Merriweather Post presents a silver-plated ticket to Vice President Hubert Humphrey, as Jim Rouse, left, and Howard Mitchell, conductor of the National Symphony Orchestra, look on. Photo by Max Araujo. Courtesy Columbia Archives.

Chapter 10:
Arts at the heart of the new town

We officially celebrate Columbia's birthday on the summer solstice, June 21, marking the day in 1967 the Wilde Lake dam was dedicated in a small ceremony.

The more formal unveiling of the new town actually occurred at a gala celebration three weeks later. On July 14, as Josh Olsen described it in his biography of Columbia founder Jim Rouse, a parade of cars brought the invited VIPs to the Town Center plaza. The crowd, in tuxedos and gowns, then made its way to the first performance of the National Symphony Orchestra (NSO) in its new summer home at Merriweather Post Pavilion, one of the first buildings Rouse had commissioned.

Vice President Hubert Humphrey was on hand to do the honors, as was Marjorie Merriweather Post, the wealthy socialite and arts patron for whom the venue is named. There were congressmen and ambassadors in the audience. (Post's family built the Mar-a-Lago estate in Palm Beach, now owned by Donald Trump.)

Before the orchestra could hit its first note, a thunderous downpour began, leaving the audience traipsing back through muddy paths to the tentless plaza. Even so, the nationally known music critic of the New York Times, Harold Schonberg, proclaimed the pavilion "an architectural and acoustical success. ... The shed is exceptionally handsome, with pleasing proportions, clean lines and an unobtrusive kind of finish that fits perfectly into the landscape."

It was a review that brought the first national acclaim to architect Frank Gehry, he would recall years later, long after his work had become world-renowned. And the review was but part of the effusive national media attention lavished on Columbia in its early years.

The event and the pavilion placed the performing arts at the heart of Columbia. For the next 50 years, Merriweather would bring hundreds of thousands of people to Columbia for music of every genre, though classical quickly took a backseat to a parade of pop artists from rock, country and folk. For many people in the region, it is their only experience of Columbia, except for the mall and the big box stores on the town's periphery.

Merriweather brought crowds, traffic, parking hassles and, depending on the group, drugs and booming noise into the night. For some of Columbia's youth, it was a first job, and for many years now, the site of high school graduations.

Now in its 50th year, the Pavilion of Music, as the planners first dubbed it, has given its name to the Merriweather District in the long-delayed completion of Columbia's downtown, an arts venue at its urban core and in its central park—Symphony Woods.

Rouse and the arts

Rouse, a leader of the Baltimore business community, knew that arts and culture were an essential element of city life, and in Columbia he was building "a real city—not just a better suburb."

As we've seen repeatedly in previous chapters, Rouse and his chief planners paid close attention to almost every detail of community life—stores and churches, bike paths and pools, schools and libraries, hospitals and colleges. The arts were no different, as witnessed by the range of topics in the Rouse correspondence files at the Columbia Archives.

There are letters and memos of meetings, not just about the National Symphony—and the Baltimore Symphony as well, which spent a few summers at Merriweather after the NSO retreated to Wolf Trap in Virginia.

There were explorations of funding with foundations and the National Endowment for the Arts. The Hirshhorn family was pursued for its modern art collection before they finally donated it to the Smithsonian and a location on the Washington mall. Washington's Corcoran School for the Arts explored setting up a campus in Columbia. A major push for funding to create the New City Ballet, a professional touring group, never succeeded, exemplifying a nagging problem for the arts in general, even for established organizations.

Internal memos went back and forth debating the visual arts center in Long Reach. What is more important, they argued, providing a space for professional artists or allowing residents to create art themselves?

It was an argument that played out over many venues—attending performances versus giving performances, viewing the arts versus creating your own art.

Jim Rouse and Wallace Hamilton, his director of institutional planning, were ready and willing to meet with most anyone who could possibly enhance the cultural presence in the planned community.

Land in Town Center near Merriweather was set aside for a professional theater. Olney Theatre and the Oregon Ridge Dinner Theatre were in competition; the more low-brow Garland Dinner Theatre won out.

Jim Rouse maintained a persistent personal interest in the presence of performing arts in the community. But the experience of owning a performance venue like Merriweather was at turns exhilarating for the level of performers it brought to the new town and frustrating for the headaches it produced. It was never a success as a concert hall for classical music, but when the rock bands arrived, it drew huge crowds of the counterculture—long hair, tie-dyed shirts and illicit drugs.

One of the most notorious concerts was the June 1970 appearance by The Who. As one clipping from a local paper recounted it: "The group's one night stand was swamped by an estimated 20,000 youths. After more than 11,000 tickets were sold, several thousand youths were admitted free when it appeared they might storm the Pavilion's fences. Only the night before, a much smaller crowd for another rock concert produced a fight resulting in numerous minor injuries and five arrests. Police called for an end to rock concerts in Columbia."

County Executive Omar Jones threatened to shut the place down, and Merriweather switched to tamer music groups, like the Doobie Brothers.

In the early 1970s, Jim Rouse scrawled a note in his signature green felt tip pen to a young Mike Spear, who eventually would become CEO of the Rouse Co. (and would die in 1990 in Boston with his wife and daughter in the crash of a plane he was piloting). Rouse was complaining about the variety of offerings at the Painters Mill Music Fair in Owings Mills—Milton Berle, the Temptations, Angela Lansbury.

"Mike, if Painter's Mill can do this, what the hell is wrong with us? (Nederlander?)," Rouse asked, referring to the New York firm that handled bookings and day-to-day operations at Merriweather.

It reflected the many challenges over the years for the pavilion as the performers and the audience changed.

Having lived in town since 1973, fighting the concert crowds on a humid summer evening has never appealed to me. But as news editor of the Columbia Flier and Howard County Times in the 1980s, I did pay attention to it as a venue for police activity. There were echoes of Merriweather's early years in the July 1985 headline "Invasion of the Deadheads," chronicling the return of the Grateful Dead. Fans slept outdoors, mall sales were up, and there were only two arrests, it reported. "There were no arrests for possession of the drugs that were widely available."

While the developer continued to fret over arts in the new town, the educated men and women who were attracted by the early promise of a planned community created cultural and arts institutions of their own—mainly the women. Many of them have come and gone. Some survive today.

Toby Orenstein

Toby Orenstein had been running a program teaching dramatics to children at the Burn Brae Dinner Theatre down Route 29 in Burtonsville after she moved to the area with her economist husband Hal Orenstein for his job in D.C. in 1959. A native New Yorker with a degree from Columbia University, she previously had taught dramatics in Harlem at P.S. 105 in a project set up by Eleanor Roosevelt.

In the early '70s, she needed to find another location. "A lot of the students were from Columbia," she recalled, including children of Rouse Co. executives, among them the vice president for leasing at the malls, Larry Wolf. In a memo to other Rouse Co. executives in the archives, Wolf urged them to attend a performance by Toby's group. They were hooked.

Orenstein had other options for her relocation, but Jim Rouse persuaded her to move from Burn Brae to the new town, where she set up the Columbia School for the Theatrical Arts. When the 1976 U.S. bicentennial rolled around, Toby formed a troupe of the youngsters to perform patriotic songs, and called them The Young Columbians. They would eventually be part of bicentennial programs in D.C. that were broadcast on TV.

The Young Columbians performed "This is My Country" at the kickoff for Columbia's birthday celebration March 19, 2017. Photo: Len Lazarick

In 1977, they performed at the White House for President Jimmy Carter's second state dinner, for Prime Minister Pierre Trudeau of Canada, father of the current PM. "In 30 minutes, they cause

American History to unfold through classic songs and dances from colonial days to the present," noted the official menu for the dinner. It was attended by Jim Rouse, an early supporter of Carter, recruited by Carter's Maryland chairman, Sen. James Clark, Jr.

(The next year, July 21, 1978, in a whirl of dust, Carter's Marine 1 helicopter would land on Clark's Route 108 farm so that the president could attend a Willie Nelson concert at Merriweather.)

By coincidence, at a Young Columbians engagement in Williamsburg, Va., Toby learned that the Garland Dinner Theatre was for sale. She bought it in 1979, and it became Toby's Dinner Theatre, putting on hundreds of musicals over the past 38 years.

"I've been very lucky, and I've been at the right place at the right time," Toby said in a 2017 interview, sitting in her cramped little office that she shares with three other people.

Toby is now on at least her eighth iteration of The Young Columbians ensemble. They performed "This Is My Country" at the March 19, 2017, kickoff of Columbia's 50th birthday celebration outside the mall.

Toby's most famous former pupil is actor Edward Norton, the grandson of Jim Rouse. In a Howard Community College Cable Eight interview in 1996, he told Carolyn Kelemen he started with Toby when he was 5 or 6 years old—that would be in the mid-1970s. By the time he was 12 or 13, he had already appeared in a couple of plays at Toby's.

He recalled Toby telling him, "You're going to make a great director some day."

Toby is planning for a reunion of The Young Columbians on June 24, and she expects 50 or 60 alumni to attend.

Still going strong at 80, with her husband Hal at her side, her dinner theater will play a major role in the development of downtown Columbia.

Columbia Pro-Cantare

On a Sunday afternoon, March 19, 2017, Frances Motyca Dawson slowly made her way to the podium at the First Evangelical Lutheran Church of Ellicott City. She was about to conduct a performance of one of her passions over the 40 years of concerts given by the Columbia Pro-Cantare chorus, which she founded in 1977—bringing the rich choral music of Eastern Europe to American audiences. For this performance, she was conducting church music by Antonín Dvořák and Zoltán Kodály, accompanied by the church's pipe organ.

Like many a classical music audience, the majority of the several hundred attendees had gray hair or no hair at all, as did the bulk of the 78-member chorus. Dawson proudly recalled one of Pro-Cantare's best-attended concerts over the decades: the 2,000-plus people who packed Holy Rosary church in 1982 in East Baltimore.

That concert of Polish music, performed at a Polish-language parish, came during the imposition of martial law in Poland after the labor unrest led by the Solidarity movement.

Like other groups that would form over the years, Dawson founded Pro-Cantare to provide opportunities both for Columbians to perform at a professional level for the auditioned but all-volunteer chorus and for residents of Columbia to experience that music. As she describes on the group's website, she was "inspired by Jim Rouse's vision of Columbia as a place where people could grow and find expression for their artistic talents."

Dawson is also proud of the 1987 Hail Columbia concert celebrating Columbia's 20th birthday that "featured Jim Rouse's premiere as a performer, when he narrated Aaron Copland's 'A Lincoln Portrait.'"

Kathie Bowen, who served as Pro-Cantare's executive director for 25 years and continues to sing as a soprano, recalled that this concert at Merriweather was sponsored by the Ryland Group, also celebrating its 20th year, as a benefit for local nonprofits. "Jim Rouse agreed [to do the performance] if Frances would coach him, which she did, and everything went off beautifully," Bowen said.

On May 14, 2017, Columbia Pro-Cantare reprised that concert with the Copland piece as well as the choral piece, Tom Benjamin's "I Build a House," in honor of Jim and Patty Rouse that opened the Jim Rouse Theatre for the Performing Arts at Wilde Lake High School in 1997.

HoCoPoLitSo

"In the early decades, there was a lot of cross-fertilization between the [arts] groups," Bowen recalled. "When I joined Columbia Pro-Cantare in 1981 and for several years afterwards, Ellen Kennedy was a member of the alto section," Bowen said. Kennedy, wife of former Columbia Association President Pat Kennedy, had been a founder of the Howard County Poetry and Literature Society, HoCoPoLitSo for short, that she initially ran out of her home next door to Jim and Patty Rouse.

Kennedy; Jean Moon, editor and general manager of the Columbia Flier; and actor Prudence Barry in 1974 founded the group, that is mostly as highbrow as its name suggests.

In April 1978, having written about Ellen Kennedy and her book on the Negritude Poets—translations of African poets who wrote in French—I was called on to introduce German poet Vincent Kling, due to my smattering of high school and college Deutsch. I joked to the audience, based on my even smaller smattering of seminary Greek, that HoCoPoLitSo sounded to me like a Greek verb meaning "to read poetry on a Saturday night."

Poetry readings are the group's stock-in-trade, and Lord knows there are few venues outside colleges and universities where poets can offer their works. Lucille Clifton was one of their favorites, a three-fer if you will—an African-American woman poet who lived in Columbia and was Maryland's poet laureate, among many other honors. She made dozens of appearances and eventually served on the HoCoPoLitSo board before her untimely death in 2010 at the age of 73.

Over the years, HoCoPoLitSo branched into fiction and drama, and even the occasional music performance, especially for its annual Irish night in February. Featured writers included big names like Isaac Bashevis Singer, Allen Ginsberg, Saul Bellow, Seamus Heaney, Edward Albee, Taylor Branch, Frank Conroy, Garrison Keillor and many lesser-knowns as well.

Last year, novelist Laura Lippman packed the Slayton House theater for a reading and discussion of her novel "Wilde Lake," which drew on her years at Wilde Lake High School.

Columbia Festival of the Arts

Researching the arts scene in and around Columbia, the name Jean Moon consistently shows up. She was the editor of the Columbia Flier in its early years, and for decades the general manager of Patuxent Publishing, and then head of her own public relations firm. She is neither an artist nor a performer, but something even more valuable in the often cash-strapped world of the arts—a patron, an engaged spectator, an appreciator, a connoisseur and a promoter.

In the decades it was running as fat as 120 pages or more, the Columbia Flier was flush with arts coverage—not just film and theater, but music, dance, the visual arts—anything from Wolf Trap in Virginia to the Mason-Dixon line. That coverage reflected Jean Moon's passion and interest.

This passion led to the founding of the Columbia Festival of the Arts as an outgrowth of the Hail Columbia experience. The brochure for its premiere program of events in 1989 said the festival "strives to bring affordable, family-oriented culture and art to Howard County." But it was also a business initiative, designed to contribute to economic development.

Over the years it consistently has brought in quality performances, such as the return of the Baltimore Symphony Orchestra to Merriweather, including some performances with Pro-Cantare. For years, big-name acts and many national and international groups performed in a 10-day extravaganza.

When Moon chaired the festival board in the 1990s, she wrote: "I think the most extraordinary thing about the arts is the emotional connection we feel with one another when we share in wonderful performances."

This was all in the context of a community that fully embraced the arts. "There was a lot of support for what other people were doing in the arts," said John Harding, arts editor of the Flier and Patuxent Publishing for 26 years until 2011. "They were a very arts-supportive community," Harding said. But "something happened to the community."

In March 2009, Nichole Hickey, director of the festival, told the Flier, "We began to see the downturn in the economy last year, in terms of financial support, in particular from the corporate side."

By that time, three of the top corporate contributors to the Columbia Festival were gone from the scene—the Rouse Co. had been sold to General Growth Properties for $12.6 billion in a move that contributed to GGP's eventual bankruptcy, the Ryland Group had moved to California, and a much thinner Patuxent Publishing was owned by the Tribune Co., also in bankruptcy. The daily Baltimore Examiner I joined in 2006 shuttered around then, and many firms struggled to survive the Great Recession.

Coverage of the arts in the Flier was severely reduced, as newspapers were on the wane, losing the common marketplace for performances. Arts consumers also had changed their behavior, impacted by a downturn in the economy and with so many more options available over cable and the Internet.

Even in prosperous times, the arts are a fragile enterprise and struggle to survive. The Howard County Arts Council and its funding has been a lifeline for many of the community groups, and the Community Foundation of Howard County (formerly the Columbia Foundation) has provided grants as well.

Before the Rouse Co. was sold, it had sought to revamp Merriweather as an outdoor venue into a much smaller theater. That led to the formation of the group Save Merriweather, including a proposal for the county to buy it.

As Jean Moon pointed out in a recent interview, "We don't have enough density [in Columbia] to be a venue for major cultural entertainment," especially with Baltimore and Washington so close. Serious patrons will travel far to sate their appetite, as the traffic jams at Merriweather attest.

An anchor at the college

As Columbia has matured, a major anchor for all the arts in the not-so-new town has been Howard Community College.

The Peter and Elizabeth Horowitz Visual and Performing Arts Center opened in 2006, becoming a cultural hub for Columbia and

Howard County. It combines performance and instruction in a sleek building built with a combination of private philanthropy and government funds.

Valerie Lash presides over it from an impressive corner office with windows and a balcony overlooking the quad that did not exist when she arrived at HCC in 1982, the longest relationship she's ever had in her life, laughed the actress and drama instructor who has always operated with flair.

"Before this building, there was no facility designed and built for instruction in the arts," said Lash, now the dean of arts and humanities at the college. The school had a commitment from the state for half of the $22 million cost of the building and was hoping to get the county to cough up the other half. But then-County Executive Jim Robey "said he could only afford half of that."

HCC began an aggressive campaign for local donors that included "salons with entertainment" Lash would organize. The Horowitzes, whose EVI Technology firm provided products and services to the National Security Agency and others, were the first million-dollar donors to the college. The unassuming couple were collectors of Russian art, and some of it is on permanent display at the college, along with a wonderful portrait of the two by faculty member James Adkins, better known in local circles for his finely detailed nudes.

HCC wound up "with benefactors for every room in the building," Lash said. Names well-known to most of the business community are attached to even small spaces such as the mostly soundproof practice rooms for musicians and studio space for painters.

A paid staff handles programming and sales for the college's two theaters, including the Smith Theater, originally a large lecture hall; and an intimate, wood-paneled recital hall, which hosted 48 concerts in the past year. "It's a business as well," Lash said. More than 50,000 patrons a year visit the facility for performances and exhibits by faculty, students and outside artists, including a Rouse Co. Foundation gallery with a rotating display of paintings, sculpture and crafts.

"I require all our faculty to be working artists, but they have to be good teachers too," Lash said.

About the only unnamed space in Horowitz is the black box theater, home to a majority of the plays by Rep Stage, founded in 1993 by Lash. "It is still the only community college in the country with a professional union theater," she said. With student productions being promoted as well, many people in Columbia and Howard County are not aware that professional-level stagecraft is offered there four or five times a year. The acting is often stellar, but the audiences for the Saturday matinees we attend are old and sparse, especially when Rep Stage takes risks with new plays, as it does most every season.

In spring 2017, the theater company staged the world premiere of a musical about black drag queens in New York, "Dorian's Closet." As off-putting as the subject matter might have seemed, the performance was masterful; the actors, mostly from out of town, had great voices, the set and costumes were superb. And the matinee, perhaps because the theme was both gay and African-American, was the largest I had seen in some time.

There are few such venues in Columbia or Howard County, which is why the Jim Rouse Theatre for the Performing Arts was attached to Wilde Lake High School as it was being rebuilt, opening in 1997 with a performance by Pro-Cantare and a dance company, and including an appearance by Rouse's grandson Edward Norton.

With 739 seats, it is still the largest professional venue in the county, though it has serious limitations.

A committee that included Lash, Moon and Orenstein also looked into the use of the former Rouse Co. headquarters as a museum and arts center. The arts community was disappointed when it became a Whole Foods supermarket in 2014.

For Toby at least, something even better has emerged in the form of the proposal for the Columbia Cultural Arts Center. It will replace the current dinner theater, which is clearly showing signs of age, but also there will be a children's theater, a parking garage, a visual arts center and more than 200 apartments, half of them affordable housing for artists. Orchard Development Corp., under chairman Earl Armiger, and the Howard County Housing Commission, under the late Tom Carbo, spearheaded the projects.

"I've been looking for my own space for a long time," Toby said in her still-thick New Yawk accent. "Howard Hughes [Corp.] has been very wonderful. I would like this to happen while I'm still alive and kicking."

The project will be next door to a revived and renovated Merriweather Post Pavilion, which just changed hands from the Howard Hughes Corp. to the Downtown Columbia Arts and Culture Commission, a nonprofit headed by Ian Kennedy, one of the leaders of the Save Merriweather citizens movement started 14 years ago.

A smaller outdoor amphitheater called the Chrysalis opened in late April 2017, a venue for performances for smaller crowds. Its lime-green brashness and location in Symphony Woods does not sit well with some long-time Columbians.

The arts and entertainment venue that launched Columbia again will be at the heart of the planned community, surrounded by an urban core of apartments and office buildings that hopefully will not complain too much when the music gets loud.

And maybe, just maybe, there will even be some nightlife in Columbia as it lurches into urbanity, with music, song and dancing to go along with food and drink, a candle that has often sputtered in the suburban darkness of a garden for growing people. In the winter of 2017, local restaurateur Steve Wecker of Iron Bridge Wine Co. plans to open a restaurant and lounge with a speakeasy theme and live music six nights a week.

And then there was ...

Delegate Terri Hill, who went on to become an Ivy League-educated plastic surgeon, asked me if I was going to write about dance teacher Anne Allen, with whom she danced when she was growing up in Columbia.

Former Business Monthly publisher Carole Pickett Ross wondered if I would be discussing the Columbia Film Society.

My copy editor mentioned I had neglected the African art museum, the institution created by Claude and Doris Ligon.

After the original article came out, an online reader was "sad to see that you missed out on reporting on the often-overlooked Columbia Bands, Inc. which has existed since 1977."

So many people, groups and organizations get left out in the limitations of time, fairly arbitrary but sensible limitations of space, and the need to create a narrative that keeps readers interested.

That has been true in most of these essays, but I feel it especially so in this piece about the arts. So many Columbians throughout these 50 years have started organizations to perform drama or song, so many have produced music and dance, so many have picked up brush and clay to shape the visual world. The potters and painters often work in solitude and are appreciated in solitude.

Dance: Carolyn Kelemen, long-time dance writer at the Flier, does a much more complete run-down of arts organizations, particularly the many dance groups, in her "Sisterhood of the New City" blog. She chronicles both the home-grown and the visiting stars who graced the stage at Merriweather and Slayton House. Kelemen also is on top of the visual arts.

Slayton House: The Wilde Lake community center was not only Columbia's first gathering place and home to its first worship services. It also has been a continuing home to community theater and dance classes, and its gallery displays the work of local artists.

Columbia Orchestra: Like Pro-Cantare, with whom it has partnered, the Columbia Orchestra began 40 years ago with volunteer musicians, and since 1999 has been under the musical direction of Jason Love, who won the American Prize for Orchestral Programming in 2013. Its audience numbered 11,000 in 2016, and it includes chamber concerts as well. The Jim Rouse Theatre is its most frequent venue.

Candlelight Concerts began in 1972, when a trio of music teachers began giving concerts at their school and brought in other artists. Under the leadership of Norm Winkler and other volunteers it incorporated in 1975, and has become a premier cultural institution presenting the best in chamber music. Over the years, the performances have featured world-class artists such as Yo-Yo Ma,

Richard Goode, the Guarneri, the Tokyo, and the Emerson string quartets. It also runs programs for children to expose them to music.

Film: Begun in 1971 at Bryant Woods Elementary School, the Columbia Film Society has been going almost as long as Columbia itself, which has a mixed history on cinema. The Smith Theatre at HCC's Horowitz Center is now the home for its series of nine independent and foreign films. It sold out its season in 2017.

The original Columbia cinema with three screens was briefly the home of independent movies beginning in 1999, but was eventually torn down for condominiums. Palace 9 north of Route 108 was eventually replaced by a Giant supermarket.

We are now left with two huge cineplexes—AMC Columbia next to the mall, and United Artists Snowden Square behind Home Depot. Both have 14 screens, comfortable stadium seating (reserved recliners at Snowden), and a wide array of food—but almost always the same mainstream films, with occasional live sports and opera.

Columbia's only museum, the African Art Museum of Maryland, began in 1980. It stayed in town as it grew through 2011, building on the collection of the Ligons. It is now located in the Maple Lawn community south of Columbia.

As to Columbia Bands, who knew? Not me, though I can't believe I haven't heard them perform, perhaps not knowing who they were. The group involves more than a hundred musicians who play various types of music for the community at no charge for the audience. It is 40 years old, and includes the Columbia Jazz Band.

Rachel Lazarick, 4, gets ready to swim at a meet in summer 1988. Photo: Len Lazarick

Chapter 11:
Recreation and the role of the Columbia Association

Three-and-a-half-year-old Rachel Lazarick jumped into the pool at the mini-meet in the summer of 1987. Despite swallowing some water, she managed to swim the 25 yards to the other end. The Owen Brown swim team coach had suggested that the young swimmer, who was taking lessons, could manage the distance. Her 7-year-old sister was already on the Barracuda team.

For the next decade or so, our family's Saturday mornings in June and July were consumed by meets of the Columbia Neighborhood Swim League. Wife Maureen Kelley would serve as clerk of the course, handing the kids those fateful cards listing their events, as well as the team manager. I would be first a timer and then, after some training, a stroke-and-turn judge. It takes about 20 to 30 adult volunteers to run your average swim meet.

As our daughters became year-round competitive swimmers in the Columbia Clippers—one of the largest USA Swimming teams in the region—there was taxiing them to daily practices, including, as they grew older, the dreaded early morning ones. There were the regional meets across Maryland and even into Virginia and Pennsylvania.

Thousands of parents and their children in Columbia have followed a similar path over the years, a tiny fraction of the population, but more than in most places due to the almost unheard-of number of pools in Columbia.

My two daughters became not just competitive swimmers but lifeguards, pool managers and coaches. Rachel went on to captain the Salisbury University swim team, and Sarai has continued to work in Columbia Association aquatics for many years, as a lifeguard trainer and auditor among other roles. It all started at the Dasher Green pool, a 10-minute walk from each of our two homes over the last 39 years.

In the swim

Columbia has 23 outdoor pools and four indoor pools. A professional study in 2001 found Columbia has about four times as many public pools as any city of its size—though it also found that Columbians patronize their neighborhood pools about five times as much as elsewhere. By comparison, Washington, D.C., six times the size of Columbia, has 36 public pools.

Each of the 10 villages, except for Town Center, an anomaly in most things, has at least one CA pool, and most of the neighborhoods of the first seven villages have a pool.

A pool open in Maryland's hot, humid summers was one of the key elements of the neighborhood concept by Columbia's planners, the essential building block of Columbia villages. As originally conceived, the neighborhood was a walkable community with an elementary school, a convenience store, a neighborhood center and a pool at its core.

As we found in chapter 6 on education, as the school board balanced county-wide interests with the school-age population, not every village would get a high school, and not every neighborhood would get an elementary school. Just a handful of the convenience stores survive, but supported by Columbia Association and its annual charge, none of the 23 pools that opened over the years have ever been permanently closed, even the one or two that have as many visitors as staff on some summer days.

No, the pools are the "center of life within Columbia," one resident told the CA board, reacting to the consultant's report recommending that one or two pools be put to a different use. What a blow to the community it would be if they closed one of those pools, a CA board member would say.

Private governance

Keeping a sports facility open that runs consistently at a big loss may seem like a poor financial decision. Yet it is completely consistent with the original philosophy behind the Columbia Park and Recreation Association. (It is not "Parks" in official documents, although that was common usage.) As Columbia got started, every one of the amenities and facilities ran at a loss, not to mention the debt it took to build them.

As discussed in chapter 5 on politics, the Columbia Association, as CPRA quickly came to be known, was a compromise over the other forms of governance that were considered. (The name officially changed in 1991.)

Remember the context. Howard County was still largely rural with a few suburban developments as Columbia planning began in 1964. The county had few urban services or public amenities. It did not have its own Recreation and Parks Department until 1969, begun that year with three people.

Jim Rouse and his firm were committed to a "garden for growing people" and building a city, not just a better suburb. They wanted to provide as many urban amenities as possible, with no added financial burden on the county government.

All the governmental forms the planners looked at—a municipality, a town, a special taxing district—couldn't accomplish what Rouse wanted on the Swiss cheese of landholdings that the company had acquired. Cities, towns and municipalities cover all the land within specific boundaries, and they can't go into debt without the current revenues to back it up.

Rouse wanted to provide recreation and community facilities to Columbians, and he and his planning team wanted some of them to be in place as residents were moving in, leveraging the financing based on the future growth. This was called preservicing.

The developer also wanted to do this without putting an immediate burden on the residents by raising the cost of land to the builders, who would simply jack up housing prices. The Rouse Co. subsidiary, Howard Research and Development, also didn't want to increase the company's own already sizable debt accumulated from buying the land, planning and building the streets, landscaping and utilities.

The Rouse Co. also wanted to maintain control of CA during the most intense development period, something it also could not do with a governmental unit run by officials chosen by the citizens. At the start, the board of directors of CA was made up entirely of Rouse Co. executives, including Jim Rouse himself. According to the charter, for every 4,000 occupied housing units, a resident representative would be added. Zeke Orlinsky, publisher of the Columbia Flier who lived then in The Cove on Wilde Lake, was the first.

Perpetual covenants

The solution to those competing goals was the Columbia Park and Recreation Association. Current CA President Milton Matthews pointed out that the Columbia Association is actually older than the official start date of Columbia, having been established in 1965, a year and a half before the new town welcomed its first residents.

As the Rouse Co. began selling land to builders or putting up apartments, stores and offices itself, it established perpetual covenants on the land. Every time land and buildings change hands in Columbia, those covenants are attached in perpetuity. With the covenants comes the lien, essentially a property tax on all residential and commercial land based on its assessment. The covenants also establish permanent architectural controls over what buildings should look like and how they can be changed.

As with most Rouse Co. planning, the role of CA, the preservicing of facilities and the architectural controls had multiple purposes. They made the community more attractive and more conducive to personal and community growth. But they also increased the value of the land that was to be sold, then and in the future. CA was a vehicle to implement social purposes, but it was also a marketing tool and a boost to the bottom line.

Jim Rouse's 1968 correspondence files show that the company paid close attention to how to explain CA to residents, going through several finely honed drafts before the brochure explaining CA was printed.

"Open space was woven throughout the city, enhancing the beauty, utility and value of homes and apartments," it said. There was "landscaping and architectural controls far beyond those normally provided."

"Architectural control assures construction of buildings throughout the city not in rigid conformity but in good taste and in harmony....[They] guarantee that the standards of design and taste that you see in Columbia today can be maintained forever."

Mounting debt

From 1965 to 1971, essentially as an arm of the developer, CA would construct the two lakes, Wilde and Kittamaqundi; the lakefront plaza; the Wilde Lake Swim Center and tennis club; the Athletic Club in Harper's Choice; the Ice Rink in Oakland Mills; Slayton House and community centers in those villages; the neighborhood pools and buildings; open space and pathways; and Symphony Woods. CA also operated a transit system, as it would for another 20 years, and provided day care and after-school care.

With only a few thousand residents and a smattering of commercial properties, its construction and operating debt continued to mount—all to be paid off in the distant future from the lien on the properties.

It was not until 1972 that CA got its first full-time president, Padraic (Pat) Kennedy, who would guide the association as it evolved over the next 26 years. Kennedy is tall, bright, charming, imaginative, a brilliant conversationalist, a respected manager and about as adept a politician as one could imagine juggling the competing interests of developer and residents in the odd governance structure that Rouse had created.

He recalled that while he was recruited by Jim Rouse himself, and would live right next door to Columbia's founder for decades, he would actually work for a board of directors that over the years had 12 different chairpersons and 77 elected village representatives, and deal with six successive Howard County executives, along with dozens of county, state and federal representatives.

He saw the best of times—and the worst of times as well.

"Columbia's success was not assured in those early days. Still there was a great sense of optimism," Kennedy wrote in an essay. "Mud was everywhere. Bulldozers were busily preparing roads and carving out sites for future homes. Signs heralded 'The Next America' and everyone knew they were part of something special."

Kennedy remembers his first years as "an explosion of creativity." More facilities were built—a visual arts center, Lake Elkhorn, a petting zoo, more child care and youth employment services. Dance floors, mirrors and ballet barres were installed in community centers.

Recession

Then in 1974, the Arab oil embargo and a deep national recession slowed Columbia development to a crawl, pushing HRD to the edge of bankruptcy. "CA almost went under," Kennedy recalled in an interview, especially as Gov. Marvin Mandel changed the property tax assessment system, reducing CA's lien income.

CA, like the Rouse Co., was forced to cut staff and operating costs and refinance its mounting debt. "The fundamental objective of the period was getting CA through the national economic crisis," said Kennedy. "They were difficult days for everyone."

I joined the Columbia Flier as associate editor in 1975, and while CA was not really part of my beat, some residents pushed for state political solutions to the problems of CA and its mounting debt.

As some residents realized, there were drawbacks to the way CA was structured—some still are, like the inflexibility of a governing structure based on land covenants. The lack of resident control over what was still an arm of the developer rubbed people the wrong way.

(Only after Kennedy arrived were the meetings of the CA board and its governing executive committee opened to the press and public. When this was first proposed in 1970, Jim Rouse in a handwritten internal memo described the prospect as "very, very dangerous." The openness and transparency of CA under Maryland's homeowner association laws is still a matter of dispute.)

As a private entity, not a governmental unit, CA also paid market interest rates on its long-term loans and bonds, at one point as high as 8–10%. Municipal bonds or even the revenue bonds from a special taxing district could be sold at much lower rates. And the lien, which operated as a property tax, was not deductible for state and federal income tax purposes—although depending on the mortgage lender, it sometimes was lumped in as a tax on escrow accounts and deducted anyway.

After months of study and debate in 1977, there was a proposal for a special taxing district that would replace CA, but the proposal died. There was some question whether a district that basically supported amenities would qualify for a tax break.

In March 1978, I wrote a long cover story for the Columbia Flier, "Is CA going broke?" (Above) It explained the whole concept of preservicing, and talked with several bond holders and financial analysts before coming to the conclusion: "If you believe Columbia will grow and prosper, the answer is NO," CA was not going broke.

HRD and CA survived in a leaner fashion. And in 1982, as Columbia development picked up and its population grew to 57,000, control of CA passed entirely to the elected representatives of the villages, where it remains today.

Organized sports

Swimming held a special place for CA, which owned most of the aquatics facilities in Howard County except for some private swim clubs. But most of the other team sports, inside Columbia and out, were played on school grounds or in school gyms.

The star of the show is the Soccer Association of Columbia/Howard County (SAC), which began in 1971 with a small loan from the Columbia Association. Soccer was a late arrival to the sports scene in the United States, but it seemed to have a special appeal to Columbians and their children. It can be played by a wide array of athletes of different sizes and abilities and of both sexes with a minimum amount of equipment.

On Facebook, many people who grew up in Columbia remember with nostalgia the early days of Columbia soccer where neighborhood teams in different colored jerseys competed against each other.

"In the early days, Columbia Maryland was the soccer capital of America," Laddie Wilson reminisced on Facebook last year. "I would not be too far wrong if I said high school soccer was as big here as high school football in Texas and basketball in New York City."

"Darrell Gee and a few other locally grown soccer players starred on the U.S. national soccer team. Columbia even had a professional soccer team!"

A 1986 interviewer asked Jim Rouse what Columbia might look like in 20 years. Rouse admitted he didn't much believe in such forecasting, but guessed that Columbia might have a soccer stadium, since "soccer will become by then a very major sport." That did not come to pass, nor did his vision for an opera house and symphony hall.

By the 1990s, there were 6,000 kids playing soccer in Columbia and Howard County. The nonprofit SAC eventually supported a small full-time staff and built its own dedicated soccer fields off Centennial Lane, in addition to the scores of sites at schools and parks.

On Memorial Day weekend, Columbia does become sort of a soccer capital, at least for the mid-Atlantic. "Here, arguably, is the heartland of U.S. soccer," a *Sports Illustrated* writer proclaimed after visiting the tournament in 1989.

There are 665 teams signed up for SAC's 42nd annual Columbia Invitational Soccer Tournament in May 2017. The tourney requires so many fields that teams will be playing not only throughout Howard County, but also in Olney, Owings Mills and the BWI area. Hotels are booked up far and wide.

Sportstown USA

Soccer is only one of the sports for which volunteers and participants have stepped up to develop clubs; there's also baseball, basketball and running. And they're not just for kids.

In 2004, Sports Illustrated dubbed Howard County a Sportstown USA, meaning it was Maryland's best community for amateur sports. At the time, the county's director of recreation and parks, Gary Arthur, estimated that 62,000 countians of all ages took part in 74 competitive sports run by 30 different groups, mostly led by volunteers.

The 34th annual Columbia Triathlon takes place in May. It started in 1983 with 90 people swimming, biking and running and now attracts upwards of 2,500 competitors. The first triathlon ended at the Columbia Swim Center in Wilde Lake, but now the race, one of the oldest triathlons in the U.S., begins with an almost mile-long swim in the county-owned Centennial Lake.

The Howard County Striders running club has been around for 40 years and has about 1,800 members. It hosts seven large races a year, mostly in and around Columbia on Sunday mornings, and many smaller events. On April 10, 2017, 626 runners finished the Clyde's 10K, among them Greg Fitchitt, vice president of the Howard Hughes Corp., the company that is redeveloping downtown Columbia. Dave Tripp, former director of investor relations for the Rouse Co., was president of the group during its early years, assisted by his wife Judy Tripp, who edited the Business Monthly for 14 years.

The Columbia Neighborhood Swim League has had its ups and downs as the villages age and the number of children decline. In 2003, 16 years after my daughters began swimming in meets at the ages of 7 and 3, they were coaching competing teams: Sarai for the Thunder Hill Lightning and Rachel for the Owen Brown Barracudas. At the suggestion of their father, who can recognize a good story, the Columbia Flier did a nice write-up about the pair headlined: "Sibling rivalry: Sisters ready teams for duel in the pool." (A photo of the article is on the next page.)

Sarai told the reporter: "I'm coaching a team that's swimming against a team that I coached for four years, who I swam on since I was 7, and again, I'm coaching against my sister, so it's a big deal."

"I've always wanted to do what she did," Rachel said. "It was never about being better. It was like, 'She's swimming, so I'm swimming; she's playing soccer, so I'm playing soccer; she's having fun, so I want to have fun.'"

Thunder Hill won. Both daughters are now public school teachers. They began learning teaching skills as teenage coaches.

Pressure on the county

As Columbia's population grew, though more slowly than projected, the county's population outside Columbia was growing as well. The number of people in the county almost doubled in the 1970s to nearly 120,000—half living in Columbia—and would grow by another 70,000 in the 1980s, increasing the demand for public parks and recreation both outside and inside Columbia. The example set by the Columbia Association led Howard Countians living outside the town to ask: "What about us?"

The Howard County Recreation & Parks Department that started 48 years ago with three employees had a full- and part-time staff of 1,271 in 2016. It maintains 9,159 acres of public lands, more than 50 parks, and offers more than 7,000 recreation programs.

In some cases, the county and CA work cooperatively, such as with the 4.6-mile Patuxent Branch trail that begins below CA's Lake Elkhorn dam and winds down to Savage. Under contract, CA also maintains many of the county-owned median strips in roadways.

Another big addition to the county's portfolio is coming online this year with the completion of phase 2 at Blandair Park, 20 years after its owner died without a will. Elizabeth Smith had refused to sell the 300 acres that straddle Route 175 in the middle of East Columbia to the Rouse Co. or other developers, and she died without signing a will she had prepared. Phase 2 adds two more lighted synthetic-turf ballfields to the three already built at the park. A new entrance road was built off Route 175.

Few residents will know or much care about the distinction between land and facilities owned by the Columbia Association, Howard County government or their school system, as long as they're available when the residents want to use them.

SPORTS

Sibling rivalry: Sisters ready teams for duel in the pool

Swimming

BY ANDREW CONRAD

Sari Lazarick, left, coaches the Thunder Hill Lightning swim team against her sister Rachel's Owen Brown Barracudas in a Columbia Neighborhood Swim League meet Saturday at the Dasher Green pool.

Staying at the top

The leadership at CA sees itself in partnership with the county government and residents in keeping up the attributes that led Money magazine to name Columbia the best small city to live in in America last September. Several times in the past decade the town had been in the top 10 of this annual ranking by editors of a publication based in New York City.

"The Columbia Association is in the quality-of-life business," said Milton Matthews, president of CA since 2014.

"I've always been interested in Columbia" since his days in grad school for urban planning, said Matthews, who held a similar post in Reston, Va., the Robert E. Simon new town in Fairfax County. "I like being here at this time during the redevelopment phase as Columbia prepares itself for the next 50 years."

Matthews said he emphasizes to CA executives that "what got you to the top is not going to leave you at the top." This means continually upgrading and improving its recreation and community facilities, a process that began some 30 years ago under Pat Kennedy.

"We're very much aware that the competition is picking up for us," said Matthews. That's among the reasons CA developed the upscale Haven on the Lake spa on the ground floor of the former Rouse Co. headquarters that's now home to Whole Foods.

Staying at the top also means maintaining the 3,600 acres of open space, three lakes, 40 ponds and 94 miles of pathways that are a key attraction for Columbia.

But Matthews and CA Board Chair Andy Stack, who's been involved in the governance of the village of Owen Brown and CA for most of the 40 years he's lived here, agree that CA also has the larger role of maintaining Jim Rouse's vision and social goals for a racially and economically diverse community.

"The social concepts are just as valuable" as the physical structure, Matthews said.

"CA is the only organization that can keep the vision alive, and keep Columbia as a planned community for the future," said Stack.

Much as the original physical planning for Columbia was designed to reinforce social goals, so CA's role in maintaining the public amenities and physical appearances goes hand in hand with promoting Rouse's goals.

CA has now paid off the heavy debt it accumulated in its first decades, and can focus on repairing, replacing and rehabilitating its existing facilities.

That also means enforcing the architectural covenants as the homes, apartments, stores, offices and commercial buildings age. The annual charge on the value of this real estate also provides almost half of CA's $77 million budget. "If you don't have redevelopment, you're dying," Stack said. "You want people to take care of their houses."

And take care of their commercial buildings as well. While the village boards and CA enforce the architectural covenants on residential property, after the demise of the Rouse Co., the covenants passed on that role for the commercial property to the Howard Hughes Corp.

There's "a great deal of interest" in taking over that covenant enforcement for Columbia's business parks, Stack said. But CA would have to add staff and procedures to do that, as well as figure out a way to pay for it.

As owner of Symphony Woods and the Kittamaqundi lakefront, CA also has intense interest in what happens to the downtown development that will increase population and assessment. "I do think Rouse envisioned higher density" there, Stack said.

"There's a role CA has to play according to the principles Jim Rouse laid down," Stack said. "There's a large focus from CA to do that."

The once two-lane Route 29 through the countryside below is now a mighty six-lane asphalt river with a wall that separates downtown Columbia from East Columbia. Photos: Above, Brent Myers Aerial Photography May 2, 2017 for Len Lazarick. Below, Courtesy Columbia Archives.

Chapter 12:
A 50-year-old town faces its future

No one had ever lived in apartment #301 at 8812 Tamar Drive in Long Reach when we moved in in June 1973. Called Bentana, it was brand-new, with two bedrooms and parquet floors. A balcony overlooked an empty field across the street where bobwhites could be heard. Rent was $200 a month, but the first two months were free, a signing bonus for the newest apartment complex in Columbia's fourth village.

Columbia was 6 years old, and Maureen and I were making a fresh start in new jobs in a new place very different from the urban commercial strip we had left in Boston's Brighton neighborhood.

We were in the South, Maureen said, and I laughed. This is Maryland. "Yes, south of the Mason-Dixon line," she pointed out. Her Rhode Island accent would mark her as a foreigner to some of the patients she would see as a visiting nurse. A native of Philadelphia, I had spent time in Baltimore, D.C. and Ocean City. Maryland was hardly the South to me, but I discovered Maureen was more right than I was once I learned more about Howard County.

We were hardly "pioneers," in Columbia lingo, those people who had moved in amid the mud and bulldozers of the new town's first 12 months. But things were still very new. The Long Reach Village Center a short walk away would not open for a year. We would wind our way over Oakland Mills Road to the little Pantry Pride supermarket in the long-gone enclosed village center, since Route 175 had not yet been built. The Mall in Columbia and the Wilde Lake Interfaith Center had just opened two years before.

The housing, the shops, the schools were fresh and modern. So were the people, like us, mostly younger couples starting families—the term baby boomer had just been coined—and even older couples in their forties with kids in high school looking for a different kind of suburb. Most, like us, were from out of state, and there was a 1960s vibe about everything in this community that was to be environmentally sensitive and open to all races, faiths and incomes living next to each other.

The new town was not about old ideas, old people, old houses, old stores, old offices, but in its 50th year that is much of what it has become.

In the original economic model, Columbia was to be completed in 1980. In earlier installments, we have seen how a recession and an oil embargo delayed the time frame. These events were accompanied by high inflation and then price controls that kept our rent steady for two years.

These factors were among the many outside forces that were not foreseen or factored into the original Columbia plans.

Women's liberation

Feminism would have to be at the top of the list of things that had not been foreseen. The planners of Columbia were all white men with traditional families. The planning work group of professors and consultants in various fields included just one woman. This was 1963, at the very beginning of the women's liberation movement in the United States, ignited by the publishing of Betty Friedan's book, "The Feminine Mystique."

An early marketing brochure for Columbia shows a large picture of a family: a "creative" wife in a dress, three kids, a dog, and a suited husband with a briefcase. The expectation was that dad would go off to work and mom would stay at home, even if she were college educated. There would be outlets for these educated "creative" wives outside of the home—pools and tennis courts, arts and crafts, and child care facilities.

And of course the stay-at-home moms would gather around the cluster mailboxes after the mail was dropped off. Really? I have heard this sexist old wives' tale—or if you prefer, "urban myth"—repeated in print and in person, as recently as last month. Maybe it was so at the beginning. I rarely saw it.

Allegedly a community-building amenity, group mailboxes were actually, as best as we can determine, an experiment by the post office to reduce the cost of delivery. By 1978, what had become the U.S. Postal Service would demand that all new suburban developments across the nation have curbside or group mailboxes; no more door-to-door delivery. A 1995 USPS study found that cluster mailboxes cut the cost of delivery per home by more than half. Now such centralized delivery is found in tens of thousands of developments across the country. My sister has one in Mesa, Ariz.

The planners' vision of domestic tranquility did not match what was going on in the culture as a whole. Columbia had to adapt to women working outside the home, the two-income household and the demand for all-day child care. Still excluded from the leadership of major business institutions—even in the forward-thinking Rouse Co. there were "men and girls"—women developed their own institutions in the arts, the media and nonprofit organizations.

"If it wasn't here, you had to start it," recalled pioneer Helen Ruther. Many of these women are now among the hundred honored in the 20-year-old Howard County Women's Hall of Fame.

The changing role of women did not come easily. Power of any kind, after all, is usually not given away but must be taken. There were many battles fought and won or lost, or a truce declared. One small but significant battle was Columbia resident Mary Stuart's fight in 1972 to keep her own name on her voter registration and her driver's license. She won the lawsuit on appeal, but married couples with separate names are still an oddity for some people and databases, as Maureen Kelley and Leonard Lazarick can attest.

The most visible success of the women's movement, as it once was called, was in Howard County politics. Women first made up a majority of the County Council in 1982. One of its members, Liz Bobo, became Maryland's first female county executive in 1986. Five women currently are among 12 state legislators, and the elected school board has been all-female for several years, except for the student member.

Few young women call themselves feminists these days, yet most have benefited from the expansion of opportunities for women brought about by the movement. On the other hand, many of the homemaking burdens of the two-income family still fall on women.

The river and the wall

A key to Rouse's plan for developing a community was maintaining control of what was placed where to build up a sense of community, land values and the bottom line. But there are so many forces outside the control of the developer—the economy, interest rates, the role of women, divorce, county politics and even the State Highway Administration.

There are two small rivers that run through Columbia, with many streams flowing into them. The big river that divides Columbia now has a wall to buttress that division. Route 29 is that asphalt river.

When Columbia began, it was a two-lane highway, with several at-grade crossings with traffic lights. In the 1970s, it became four lanes. In 1992, the last traffic light was replaced with Broken Land Parkway overpasses connecting east and west. Now there are six lanes, often choked with rush hour traffic due to the building of high sound barrier walls along its east side. The cars come mostly from outside Columbia.

Most of the important institutions in Columbia are west of the Route 29 river. The iconic images of Columbia are taken looking west over Lake Kittamaqundi, the way the first model for the new town shown to Howard County residents was photographed. From "The People Tree" and the fountain on the lakefront plaza; to Columbia's first office buildings and exhibit center; to Symphony Woods and Merriweather; to the first village center, the community college and the hospital, all are west of Route 29. Rouse executives and many of its first community leaders lived west of the Route 29 river, as well, and now there's a wall.

In that original model, there is a bridge across the highway, seeming to connect to the Oakland Mills Village Center, the most isolated of the struggling centers. Instead, Route 175 and Broken Land Parkway cross the river. The pedestrian bridge from Oakland Mills is slated to be improved, but it only connects to downtown by foot or by bike, which is not how most residents travel back and forth.

Seldom do we see the view looking east depicted. It is most assuredly green until you hit Dobbin Road and Snowden River Parkway. On the edges of this greenery that make up the villages of

Oakland Mills, Long Reach and Owen Brown are the big box stores and the bulk of Columbia's employment centers. The BJ's, Wegmans, Wal-Mart, Apple Ford and other car care outlets, along with the business parks, are arguably as important institutions to many residents as most anything in Town Center.

Then again, Rouse's notion was that people would be more conscious of living in neighborhoods, connected at their core by a village center with all the essential services—except the gas stations in Wilde Lake and Oakland Mills are long-gone. People can't go much of anywhere without a car, and if they don't leave Columbia, they pay some of the highest gas prices in the Baltimore region.

Commuting

A core Rouse ideal was that people of all ages, backgrounds and incomes would live and work in Columbia. That ideal couldn't survive the patterns of work and housing in post-industrial Maryland—or the success of the new town itself, even in its early years.

On Columbia's sixth birthday in June 1973, the month Maureen Kelley and I moved in, editor Jean Moon wrote the Columbia Flier cover story bemoaning the lack of the promised diversity.

"Where are our 'blue collar' workers, those 2,700 men and women who work at General Electric, located in the town with the 'sound economic base.' Where are the 6,500 construction workers who are building this city?" Moon asked.

"They are not here," she went on. "Not in Columbia where more than one out of four residents has completed post-graduate work. They are not among the doctors, dentists, lawyers, engineers, architects, planners and government employees who comprise the majority of our working population."

This is the city that Jim Rouse said would provide "houses and apartments at rents and prices to match the income of all who work here, from company janitor to company executive," she wrote.

Moon critiqued the rapid rise in housing values that allowed the early settlers to make a killing on their low-priced townhomes and move on to something bigger and better—further putting housing prices out of the reach of middle incomes.

"We are so successful that we are really a failure," Moon said. Not much has changed in 44 years, except the need for two incomes to afford to live here.

The notion that most of these professionals would somehow work in Columbia was never true. Today, at least two-thirds if not more of employed Columbia residents have commutes of greater than 15 minutes. This means they travel to work somewhere outside the boundaries of Columbia in a region with some of the worst commutes in the country. As in the past, many people work at the National Security Agency in Fort Meade or its contractors, or at Social Security in Woodlawn, or in Baltimore, or in the Washington suburbs and even the capital itself. Rush hour traffic jams near NSA are routine.

Tens of thousands more employees flow into Columbia's business parks from elsewhere in the region. Many of these non-Columbia residents will not tread too far off the major roads to venture into the Columbia villages, lest they get lost in the loop streets and maze of cul-de-sacs with funny names.

Jim Rouse himself commuted to Columbia from Baltimore until he bought a home in 1974. Columbia pioneers planning their 50th birthday reunion laugh recalling the debate about whether the non-resident Rouse should be invited to their fifth birthday get-together. Columbia now has its own suburbs in Clarksville and Ellicott City. Maple Lawn just south of Columbia could be mistaken for another Columbia village.

County officials, the Columbia Association, the Howard Hughes Corp. and many others still struggle with finding ways to provide affordable housing for even middle-income teachers, cops and residents without the federal housing subsidies that fostered Columbia's housing mix in its early years. Attracted to the new town's cheapest housing, many minorities sacrifice much to buy and rent in Columbia for its better schools, or use their Section 8 vouchers.

The housing bubble of the early 2000s followed by the housing bust in the Great Recession did not help the cause to make living here affordable.

Retail hurricane

The turmoil in retailing has been going on for decades. Columbia's village centers were once dominated by small merchants and supermarkets, some of them locally owned. (Giant, once dominant in the region, is now part of a Belgian corporation.) All of them are threatened by discount grocers and warehouse stores, like Wal-Mart and Costco. The original Columbia supermarkets were not built large enough for all the special services the modern chains needed to add.

The biggest changes are in the regional shopping malls that Rouse pioneered, that helped to kill the downtown department stores that once flourished in big cities till their customers moved to the suburbs.

Urban historian Howard Gillette wrote that Columbia has been "described, accurately enough, as a city built around a shopping mall." Rouse rejected the advice of his own planners to locate the mall near I-95. He envisioned it central to the town, as Columbia's Main Street. In its first decade, it was full of local merchants and community activities.

On Facebook pages, Columbians and folks who grew up here wax nostalgic about hanging out at the mall or getting their first job there. But malls have been constantly evolving. Three of the four anchor department stores at the Mall in Columbia—Sears, J.C. Penney and Macy's—are struggling to survive the Internet wave and competition of the big box stores the Rouse Co. would build here. Two of the mall's original anchors are gone, and Macy's is the third occupant in that same building. Sears recently closed its top floor.

The Rouse Co. had for decades gained most of its revenue from its national network of shopping malls, a source of some resentment in the company where Columbia got much of the spotlight. Rouse executives probably picked an excellent time in 2004 to sell the business, given the trends in retailing since.

Once at the center of community life, the Mall in Columbia is now a hub of commercialism surrounded by a sea of parking lots. The latest trend in urban planning is for more mixed-use development—mixing apartments, shops and civic uses together as seen in the revamped Wilde Lake Village Center, the Metropolitan apartment complexes near the mall and the future plans for the Merriweather District.

The mall, which Jim Rouse considered one of his company's best, was one of the key selling points to the women who already lived in Howard County when Rouse first pitched his idea for a new city. Given its location and its affluent market, it seems likely to survive the shuttering of regional malls across the country.

Mostly safe but still crime

In January 2014, the mall bounced back quickly from its worst calamity, the fatal shooting of three people, including the suicide of the gunman. What the incident revealed, among other things, was how well the Howard County police and its young, Columbia-born executive Ken Ulman responded to a crisis that was blasted across the national news. It gave Columbia more, but more negative, coverage than it had received in decades. It also disclosed that the county police had quietly practiced shelter-in-place drills with mall personnel that would have saved lives in a worse shooting incident.

For many Columbia residents, crime has no place in any narrative of their time here. "One of the advantages of Columbia is that you feel safe," said Ethel Hill, a longtime resident, activist and former Columbia Association board member who moved here from West Philadelphia in 1969.

As the news editor of the Flier and Howard County Times for four years in the 1980s, crime was one of the beats I supervised—murder, rape, assault, robbery, embezzlement, drug busts, child abuse, all occurred at one time or another. My late mother once told me she didn't read newspapers because they contained so much bad news. Sorry, Mom, but that's what we do.

I once had to tell a new Flier reporter that there had been a change in plans, and she was being switched to the cops beat. She broke down in tears. At a previous job, she had been traumatized by covering a murder that she could smell as she approached the victim's house.

Howard County Executive Ken Ulman talks to reporters with Gov. Martin O'Malley and police officials at his side as the mall reopened after the fatal shooting. Governor's Office photo by Jay Baker.

Columbia indeed is safer than many places, and certainly safer than North Philly where I went to high school or West Baltimore where my wife has seen patients for years. But besides my professional connection supervising cops and courts coverage, crime has hit close to home.

In October 1985, a Washington Post distributor was stabbed to death in the early morning hours outside the High's convenience store next to the Dasher Green pool where we all spent so much time. We didn't get our Post that day. Police soon arrested the 19-year-old who had left a note on the body taunting them. He lived in our neighborhood a short walk away.

Less than a year later, there was another murder with much closer personal connections. Aruna Mittal was suffocated in her home, where she had provided day care for my daughters until just a few weeks before. Her husband first claimed it was a robbery gone bad, a report that set the neighborhood on edge. It turned out her husband actually did the crime, as part of an affair with Aruna's sister who lived with them. When Maureen and 6-year-old Sarai attended the funeral, they didn't realize they would be seeing their first Hindu cremation.

Our current house was broken into before Christmas the following year. No one was home. The audio system and some Christmas gifts were stolen. I regretted not having installed the bars over the basement window that the thieves had crawled through. The police investigated, and eventually arrested two teens who lived on the next cul-de-sac. Columbia's wooded pathways have many uses.

In 2005, my 3-month-old Honda Accord was stolen from our driveway during the night. The owner had stupidly left the valet key in the center console; otherwise, the car thieves might not have been able to drive it off after breaking in. A day or two later, the speeding car, with five people inside, was involved in a high-speed police chase up Route 29 and onto Route 40 toward the Patapsco State Park. The occupants eventually bailed out by the park, fleeing into the woods. State Farm wound up paying $12,000 to repair the almost-new car.

From the fingerprints, Howard County police eventually tracked down all five occupants of the car, all Columbians, a couple of them juveniles. As a victim, I got to witness my first juvenile hearing for one of the boys, clad in orange jumpsuit and chains. Nabbing all the males involved was a surprise. A bigger surprise came months later when I got a check from the state as restitution for the items stolen from the car.

Making lemonade

I could go on and on about the things in Columbia that went wrong, weren't planned or didn't succeed. The bad news my mother avoided.

That was not Jim Rouse's way, as he reminded us at a lunch on Founder's Day at the community college on May 9, 2017, organized to discuss the developer and his vision with the Rouse scholars, the college's honors students. On film, he related the oft-told story of the first meeting of the Work Group in 1963. Round and round the experts at the table went, telling him how and why his city for growing people wouldn't work and couldn't work. The same happened the second day, until finally one of the group said, wait a minute, aren't we talking about fostering love in a community? And the whole tenor of the discussion changed.

"Everybody comes with a vested negative," Rouse tells the video interviewer. In an earlier video, we had heard Rouse say, "The development business is one of managing crises. ... There's no such thing as an adverse event." It's how it is handled that counts, he said.

That's why, on the wall of his office, Rouse had a framed poster of the now-familiar saying popularized by Dale Carnegie: "When life gives you lemons, make lemonade." Rouse was forever making lemonade, adding sugar and ice to many situations, and selling it to people who couldn't believe how quenching it was.

A series of interviews with many of the early settlers by a University of Maryland anthropology class in 2015 found them no less enthusiastic.

"Interviewed residents, regardless of when they first moved in, agreed that Rouse's original vision and goals remain important for Columbia. Some expressed a concern that the goals have weakened over time due to rapid population growth, increased emphasis in pursuing profit over growing people, and larger changes in society," their report found.

"Residents cited increasing traffic congestion, the technology revolution, better understandings of the natural environment, rising housing prices, generational turnover, and new incoming populations as areas Columbia will need to address in planning ahead for the future."

The students found that "many newcomers didn't know about Rouse's vision or goals until they were brought up in interview." While the social goals were more elusive, the dedication to the environment and open space won some over, despite earlier misgivings.

Adam Herson moved to Columbia at the end of 2012 after repeated visits to a friend there.

"I didn't like just about everything about Columbia," he said. "You pretty much had to drive everywhere. The fact that you couldn't find anything. There are no signs." Over time, Herson became impressed that "pretty much everywhere is nothing but green."

That respect for the land led to 94 miles of pathways through streambeds and woods that actually establish most of the boundaries of Columbia's 10 villages and 32 neighborhoods—its basic building blocks.

Harvard urban design professor Ann Forsyth, who has studied Columbia for many years, said this open space planning "took advantage of the strengths of the rural landscape but has made the shape of each neighborhood and village difficult to perceive from the ground, because the edges are literally buried in trees."

In almost any aerial view of Columbia, even its densest Town Center, the buildings are always poking out of trees. First-time foreign visitors often remark how green it is.

"Open space is probably one of the major successes of Columbia," environmental author Ned Tillman said. "Many cities and towns did not do a good job of that."

Forsyth returned to Columbia for Founder's Day, with a new focus on creating healthy environments from urban design. Her studies have found that the greenery display not far from most any doorstep in Columbia is good for mental health, not just the physical health of walkers, joggers and bikers. "Rouse instincts were pretty good," Forsyth said.

Cherishing diversity

It is the socio-economic, racial, ethnic and religious diversity that Columbia's longer residents most cherish, as does Dr. Terri Hill, who represents west Columbia in the House of Delegates.

Ethel Hill's daughter moved to the Running Brook neighborhood with her parents in 1969 when she was 10. Her father worked at Social Security in Woodlawn, as many Columbians still do. Her older sister Donna, who would eventually become a judge and deputy attorney general, was among the first students at the new Wilde Lake Middle School and then the Wilde Lake High in Columbia's first village. Both schools were innovations designed to operate in the round. Both have been replaced, the middle school in 2016 as a solar-powered building. In the round, some students flourished and others languished.

"By the time I got [to high school], we had schedules, but you were still working at your own pace," said Terri Hill.

Hill, who is African-American, threw herself into Columbia's opportunities—the winter swim league, dance classes, lifeguarding, using the Call-a-Ride system to get around. She was president of her Wilde Lake High class in her junior and senior years.

She went off to Harvard and then Columbia University for medical school, and Columbia-Presbyterian Hospital for a residency in plastic surgery.

"When you leave Columbia and start dealing with people from other places, you realized how different Columbia is," said Hill, who returned in 1991. "I still think Columbia is something special."

Her high school classmates get together for reunions every five years, and "a lot of them live in Columbia. ... My closest friends are still in Columbia," Hill said. Many of them left and came back as she did.

Newcomers to Columbia are different from those early decades. "People come for the amenities and not [for] a community based on a shared ethics and values," Hill said. Like many of the old-timers, she mourns the long-gone Exhibit Center where new arrivals would learn of Rouse, his goals and housing opportunities.

"I think it's still striving to be that community with very unique beliefs in socio-economic, ethnic religious mix. I do think it works toward those goals."

The 50th birthday events a coalition of community organizations is sponsoring seek to remind Columbia residents of what the planned community was supposed to be.

Reminders also take place on Facebook and in blogs and private chats.

A typical comment came from Tricia McDonaugh in 2016: "I just want to take a moment to say how privileged I feel to have grown up in Columbia. My own children are mixed race and we have lived in the south and north. When they began school, I thought it was imperative that they live in Columbia. We were and still are the fishbowl of America. I'm so proud to raise my children in a place where skin color and religion are not a reason for judgment."

McDonaugh's post drew scores of positive comments like Kim O'Malley's: "You knew you grew up in Columbia when ... Your mom was a Russian Jew and your Father was Irish Catholic and in high school your boyfriend was black and you NEVER experienced racism until you moved to another state as a grown up."

In 2016, Money magazine rated Columbia as the best place to live in America. The town had been among the top 10 for a decade, providing the kind of external validation Columbia used to get in its early years. "I think we all knew before Money magazine that this was a wonderful place to live," said Del. Vanessa Atterbeary at the mall kickoff for Columbia's 50th. She is a lawyer who was born and raised in Columbia, and now represents part of it.

Where it ends

Where to end this long walk down memory lane?

One way is a drive down Route 108 toward Clarksville. Cross the Middle Patuxent River, still a stream valley, not a lake as originally envisioned. Up the hill on the left is Columbia Memorial Park.

There are four small historic cemeteries surrounded by development in Columbia, but the official Columbia cemetery is not in Columbia at all. In the late 1970s, I once casually asked Jim Rouse, as we chatted before an interview, why there was no cemetery in Columbia. With my armchair psychology, I envisioned some attempt by Rouse to deny death by avoiding its repository. His parents died when he was a teenager and his siblings all died young. Instead, Rouse told me the numbers didn't work—Columbia land was too valuable for use as a final resting place. Cemeteries are businesses, too.

The 38-acre Columbia Memorial Park opened in 1988. Like many modern cemeteries, the grave markers are ground-level metal plaques. A number of gravesites, like the Rouses', have low-slung stone benches with the family name.

Five miles from his home on Wilde Lake, Jim Rouse lies buried with his second wife Patty. Jim died April 9, 1996, two weeks before his 83rd birthday and 17 years after he left the company that bore his name. Patty lived on another 16 years, dying March 3, 2012. They lived full lives of great accomplishment.

A short walk back towards the woods is another more poignant gravesite with three markers: Michael David Spear, Judith Sue Spear, Jodi Lynn Spear. They all died Aug. 24, 1990, when the plane Mike was piloting crashed in Boston with his wife and a daughter aboard. Mike had just turned 49 and was president of the Rouse Co., where he had worked since 1967 on the Columbia project, living modestly in a Wilde Lake townhouse and raising their family.

"Mike Spear was a brilliant, compassionate, wise man," Rouse said. "In many respects, he is irreplaceable." Many of us would agree with Rouse and wonder what might have happened to Columbia in that decade if Spear had lived.

Jim Rouse and Mike Spear may be buried there, but the story doesn't end there. There is a brief inscription on Rouse's grave marker: "We raise up rational visions. What ought to be can be."

What ought to be, can be. Rouse said it often, and it has been repeated many times by acolytes and admirers. It reflects his optimism and his consistently aspirational rhetoric. Without his aspirations, his noble aims, how could he conceive of building a city— "a garden for growing people"—on 14,000 acres of Howard County farmland?

But Rouse was also a realist. How could a mortgage banker turned shopping mall developer not be tethered to the realities of topography and interest rates, material costs and time?

Time is not kind to stick-built homes, or once fashionable shopping centers. The new structures of Columbia's heyday are now old; the new families who lived in them are getting old as well.

Maturation planning

In her keynote address at Founder's Day, Harvard professor Ann Forsyth pointed out Columbia was part of the first golden age of new towns in the 1960s. More than 115 planned communities of more than 30,000 people were started around the world. Like Columbia, they are now reaching middle age and need to address their aging.

But now, around the world, "we're in the midst of another new town golden age," especially in urbanizing China, where 111 new towns were started in the last decade.

"Columbia still stands out as one of the most admirable new towns in terms of its overall planning," Forsyth said. Columbia represents an important model, even though Jim Rouse "couldn't create a General Motors of city building."

Even in the 1980s, it was recognized that few entities could assemble this much undeveloped land with financiers patient enough to wait decades for a return on their investment.

Yet in the planning literature, Columbia is still one of the most cited developments, Forsyth said, and it could be that again as it deals with "maturation planning," moving beyond the initial vision. Maturation planning "has not been done very well" most places, she said. "Columbia could be a real leader because Columbia has always been forward looking."

While Howard County grew around and west of Columbia in the 1990s, the planned community largely expanded commercially on its eastern edge and residentially in River Hill. That village will forever remain disconnected from the rest of West Columbia since Little Patuxent Parkway does not cross the Middle Patuxent.

Except for some garden apartments and townhouses built near the mall on land once planned for offices, Town Center had been largely stagnant till the last few years.

The planner's job is much harder now. There is no master developer like the Rouse Co. owning thousands of empty acres. With no one else in charge, Howard County government and the Columbia Association are the only institutions with a broader view of the public interest. Neither have the imagination or power Jim Rouse possessed to execute his innovations. The institutions he fostered or imagined are now powers in their own right.

Unlike green pastures and cornfields with a few farmhouses and scattered suburbanites, there are thousands of Columbia residents with firm views on what the town's future should look like. Pioneers were not voiceless but they had to reach only a few ears, not cajole multiple power centers.

Many of them call on the legacy of Jim Rouse as they choose to interpret it. "One of the unique things [about Columbia] is that it has a founder and a patron saint," Rouse biographer Josh Olsen told the Founder's Day audience.

WWJD?

WWJD? What would Jim Rouse do? The gospel according to Jim Rouse is subject to many interpretations. One of the claims is that Rouse did not plan for urban density.

In a long 1986 video interview, Rouse was asked what Columbia would be like in 20 years.

"I don't believe much in these kinds of distant views of what it" will be, Rouse said. Nevertheless, he went on:

"Columbia will become in 20 years clearly the third major city in the Columbia-Washington corridor. What will be called Columbia—which means Columbia and its developed environs—will be a city of, oh, 300,000 people, maybe more, maybe half a million." (Howard County's entire population in 2017 is approaching 320,000.)

He also said there will be six department stores, an opera house, a symphony hall, a stadium for soccer, which "will become by then a very major sport," said Rouse. And of course, "there ought to be a livelier downtown."

Rouse at that point had become more famous for developing festival marketplaces in downtown Boston and Baltimore, repurposing the historic Faneuil Hall and the once-decaying Inner Harbor waterfront.

What about the awful prospect of high-rise office buildings? Surely Jim Rouse, of the white stucco four-floor headquarters building on Lake Kittamaqundi, now a Whole Foods, would not have approved. Then you discover his 1966 letter to Connecticut General proposing to erect a 300–500-foot office building, with a restaurant on top where diners might catch a glimpse of the Baltimore or Washington skyline. That's 25 to 40 stories, 10 to 15 stories taller than anything currently planned. Connecticut General said no, and no more was heard of it.

Would Jim Rouse have approved the stunning new lime green Chrysalis stage in Symphony Woods, its hue called "Greenery," named Color of the Year by the Pantone Color Institute? Who knows? Except we might note that Michael McCall, who led the work on the Inner Arbor development, worked closely with Rouse in his final career at Enterprise Development. And Rouse, way back when, had painted his own front door yellow without asking the permission of the Wilde Lake architectural committee.

McCall pointed to the results of a three-year Knight Foundation Soul of the Community study done with the Gallup polling folks, who surveyed residents in 26 communities—cities small, medium and large. The study focused on the emotional side of the connection between residents and their communities.

The newest office buildings in downtown Columbia, where none had been built for 15 years. Above, Little Patuxent Square, a nine-story mixed use complex with offices in front, ground floor retail and luxury apartments behind it with views of Lake Kittamaqundi. Below, the MedStar Health building at Little Patuxent and Broken Land parkways. There is another building going up behind, the first in the new Merriweather District. Photos: Len Lazarick

"What attaches residents to their communities doesn't change much from place to place," said the study. "While one might expect the drivers of attachment would be different in Miami from those in

Macon, Ga., in fact the main drivers of attachment differ little across communities. Whether you live in San Jose, Calif., or State College, Pa., the things that connect you to your community are generally the same," said the study's summary of its findings.

"When examining each factor in the study and its relationship to attachment, the same items rise to the top, year after year:

• Social offerings—Places for people to meet each other and the feeling that people in the community care about each other

• Openness—How welcoming the community is to different types of people, including families with young children, minorities, and talented college graduates

• Aesthetics—The physical beauty of the community including the availability of parks and green spaces."

"Interestingly, the usual suspects—jobs, the economy, and safety—are not among the top drivers. Rather, people consistently give higher ratings for elements that relate directly to their daily quality of life: an area's physical beauty, opportunities for socializing, and a community's openness to all people."

"Remarkably, the study also showed that the communities with the highest levels of attachment had the highest rates of gross domestic product growth. Discoveries like these open numerous possibilities for leaders from all sectors to inform their decisions and policies with concrete data about what generates community and economic benefits."

Columbia is already way ahead on the most important factors. Of course, McCall sees the Chrysalis project, and overall revamping of the Merriweather District, contributing to both socializing and aesthetics, and an appeal to Millennials. A vocal minority of Columbians disagrees.

Terri Hill is not thrilled with some of the new downtown development just beginning in the Merriweather District, the new MedStar building for one. She believes Columbia has "the best of urban living and the best of suburban living."

"Columbia doesn't want to be Bethesda," Hill said. "If Columbia is not urban enough for you, then go move to another place."

Thousands of property owners of homes and businesses must also be encouraged to update, improve and rehabilitate their aging structures, or even forced to do that if the decline is bad enough. A healthy, 40-year-old tree is a nice amenity; a 40-year-old house that has been neglected is not. The village associations and CA have some power to force upkeep, and CA is studying taking over responsibility for the business parks and commercial areas where Howard Hughes Corp. still has nominal control, though not ownership.

There are concerns that property values are at risk, but a 2013 CA study of market trends found: "Residential sales prices in Columbia's villages have fared well in the past decade even with the 'great recession' of 2008 to 2009. ... In general, the percentage increase in average sales prices for the Columbia villages were equivalent or exceeded those for Howard County for the years between 2001 and 2007 and fell less steeply than those in the county in 2008 and 2009."

A more recent 2017 study for the always-struggling Oakland Mills Village Center and environs found the housing market there was "at a stage of general value stability relative to the surrounding regional market, with prices moving more or less in tandem with other locations." Home prices were sometimes lower there because the houses were smaller.

There is wild talk of a used car lot at Route 108 and Red Branch Road, and how awful that might be. Presumably, those residents get around town on foot or by bike and are appalled by the huge Apple Ford complex on Snowden River Parkway, used cars and all.

With little but acreage in downtown (and some in Gateway) in control of Howard Hughes, the county has taken the lead. First steps have been taken to make Gateway into an "innovation center." It is now as bland and un-Columbia-like as any office park in the region, but could it be transformed into another Columbia neighborhood with mixed uses on some still-vacant lots, or redevelopment of one-story flex office buildings? The county is also asking the state to look at better access from I-95.

189

There is even more concrete hope for the Long Reach Village Center, with more apartments and townhouses. Orchard Development Corp. is taking the lead as it has for Toby Orenstein's part of Merriweather District.

While the town may be turning 50, and a quarter of its residents are 55 or older, another quarter of its residents are 19 or younger. There's a lot of young blood in the aging new town if they can be enticed to stay here.

The Founder's Day event at Howard Community College concluded with a short video clip from Jimmy Rouse offering the typical Rouse-like uplift.

His father, said Jimmy, "was not into being a hero or saint. He was into the growth of human potential."

"He was a deeply spiritual person" who believed that "we are co-creators with God," Jimmy told several hundred people in the Smith Theatre, mostly an over-50 crowd.

"You all are co-creators with him of Columbia. It is for you all to go out and create this great city."

Columbia has been for me and many a great place to live, work, thrive, raise a family and even die. Can it be that great city in the future?

It's in our hands and in the hands of a generation to come.

Afterword and Acknowledgements

I began thinking about this book at least 12 years ago, but for years it was simply a folder on my desk with some ideas stuck in it. In January 2016, the 50th Birthday fast approaching, I realized I had to find a way to write and publish a book that would force me to get it out by June 2017.

I thank my friends at the Business Monthly, Publisher Becky Mangus and General Manager Cathy Yost, for enthusiastically embracing my pitch to them of 12 months of articles. I must also thank them for enlisting long-time Special Sections Editor Joan Waclawski to edit the copy. She is meticulous and thoughtful, but not heavy handed. Joan made many good suggestions.

I also want to thank the 10 organizations that sponsored the series in the Business Monthly. They made it financially possible for me and the newspaper to do the series and give it a wider audience. Most are mentioned in this book because they have played significant roles in Columbia's past and are planning to do the same in the future. They had no prior review of its content.

Those Business Monthly sponsors were: The Columbia Association, the Merriweather Post Pavilion, Orchard Development Corp., the Creig Northrop Team, Howard Bank, Harkins Builders, Howard County Economic Development Authority, the Horizon Foundation, the Howard Hughes Corp., and Toby's Dinner Theatre.

You cannot write about Columbia, especially its early days, without the help of the Columbia Archives and its director Barbara Kellner. She has helped in many ways, as has her assistant Jeannette Lichtenwalner, especially with the photos. The Columbia Archives, and its parent, the Columbia Association, are really the only ways the founding spirit of Jim Rouse can stay alive as the pioneers and early settlers die off.

I talked to more than 50 people on various topics for this book. Many were old friends and acquaintances that made it a pleasure to do the research. Most of these are mentioned in the chapters that they contributed to, so I will not list them all here. With many of them, I had conversations over lunch or coffee rather than interviews in order to jog my memory and clarify my thoughts. There were some people whom I did not know well who also were interviewed, and they are acknowledged in the chapters as well.

I appreciate all the positive comments and feedback I've received online, in emails and in person. That includes the ones that said: "I liked what you wrote, but…" Some of the "buts" made it into the book.

Mistakes

There are surely some mistakes in this book. As it was rolled out over 12 months in the Business Monthly and MarylandReporter.com, I've tried to correct those that were brought to my attention. If you find others, you may go online to MarylandReporter.com, find the part that corresponds to the chapter number and make a comment with a correction or some additional details. Or send me an email at Len@MarylandReporter.com, and I will make the comment.

The 12 parts on MarylandReporter.com are 95% of what appears in the book. There are also more photos, and they are in color.

There are many omissions in this book. Many, many people who contributed to life in Columbia have been left out. Many events have been overlooked, and many subjects not covered in detail. That's why it was called a "memoir." It is historical, but it is my interpretation of that history. Written over 12 months, it was limited by the time and space available. If you find someone or something that should really be mentioned, please add a comment to that part online.

There is also no index, and there are no footnotes. As a writer, I like to look for names and topics in indexes, too, but it just wasn't feasible. Besides running out of time to do an index, I couldn't figure out a way that would be useful. I hope the organization of the book is helpful. Ten of the chapters are topical, most are fairly short, and they all have subheads to make finding things easier.

About the Author

Len Lazarick has lived in Columbia, Md., since 1973. Len is currently editor and publisher of MarylandReporter.com, a news website about state government and politics he founded in 2009 as a nonprofit corporation with foundation funding. He is also a political columnist at the Business Monthly.

He was formerly the State House bureau chief of the daily Baltimore Examiner from its start in April 2006 to its demise in February 2009.

In 1975, Len became the first associate editor at the Columbia Flier. In the 1980s, Len was State House chief and political editor of Patuxent Publishing, then a chain of 13 weeklies that included the Flier. From 1988 to 1996, he was managing editor of Patuxent Publishing's nine Baltimore County papers where he headed a staff of 30 editors, reporters and editorial assistants. Those papers, like most newspapers, are now emaciated versions of their former selves, with fewer pages and a decimated staff.

In 1997, he was senior associate producer at Maryland Public Television for C-Span-style coverage of State House hearings. From 1998 to 2006, Len was on the national copy desk of the Washington Post. At the same time, he spent eight years as the news editor and political columnist for The Business Monthly circulating in Howard and Anne Arundel counties. He also edited the Trustee Quarterly for the national Association of Community College Trustees.

In 1984–85, on leave from the Flier, Len spent 10 months as an editor at the International Herald Tribune in Paris. He has taught Asian history at Montgomery College, Md., and state and local government at Howard Community College.

He is past president of the Maryland Chapter of the Society of Professional Journalists, and is a member of both the Maryland and D.C. chapters of SPJ and a member of the National Newspaper Association.

Len has a bachelor's degree in history from Boston College and a master's degree in East Asian history from the University of Maryland College Park.

CPSIA information can be obtained
at www.ICGtesting.com
Printed in the USA
BVOW11s0110080617

486346BV00005B/10/P